General editor: Graham Handley MA Ph.D.

Brodie's Notes on Philip Larkin's
# Selected Poems

Graham Handley MA Ph.D.
Formerly Principal Lecturer in English, College of All Saints, Tottenham

MACMILLAN

# For Pat and Sophie, with love

ACKNOWLEDGEMENTS I am particularly grateful to
Anne Dangerfield for her help with this study.

The publishers wish to thank The Marvell Press for permission
to quote from poems first printed in *The Less Deceived* (1955),
and Faber & Faber Ltd for permission to quote from poems
first published in *The Whitsun Weddings* (1964)
and *High Windows* (1974), reproduced in *Collected Poems
by Philip Larkin*, edited by Anthony Thwaite (1988).

First published by James Brodie Ltd
This revised edition first published 1991
by Pan Books Ltd

Published 1994 by
THE MACMILLAN PRESS LTD
Houndmills, Basingstoke, Hampshire RG21 2XS
and London
Companies and representatives
throughout the world

ISBN 0-333-58138-5

Printed in Great Britain by
Cox and Wyman Ltd
Reading, Berkshire

# Contents

References in these Notes are to the Collected Poems of Philip Larkin, edited by Anthony Thwaite, The Marvell Press and Faber and Faber but references are also given to the original publications, so that these Notes may be used with any edition of the poems.

# Preface by the general editor

The intention throughout this study aid is to stimulate and guide, to encourage your involvement in the book, and to develop informed responses and a sure understanding of the main details.

Brodie's Notes provide a clear outline of the play or novel's plot, followed by act, scene, or chapter summaries and/or commentaries. These are designed to emphasize the most important literary and factual details. Poems, stories or non-fiction texts combine brief summary with critical commentary on individual aspects or common features of the genre being examined. Textual notes define what is difficult or obscure and emphasize literary qualities. Revision questions are set at appropriate points to test your ability to appreciate the prescribed book and to write accurately and relevantly about it.

In addition, each of these Notes includes a critical appreciation of the author's art. This covers such major elements as characterization, style, structure, setting and themes. Poems are examined technically – rhyme, rhythm, for instance. In fact, any important aspect of the prescribed work will be evaluated. The aim is to send you back to the text you are studying.

Each study aid concludes with a series of general questions which require a detailed knowledge of the book: some of these questions may invite comparison with other books, some will be suitable for coursework exercises, and some could be adapted to work you are doing on another book or books. Each study aid has been adapted to meet the needs of the current examination requirements. They provide a basic, individual and imaginative response to the work being studied, and it is hoped that they will stimulate you to acquire disciplined reading habits and critical fluency.

Graham Handley 1991

# The author and his work

Philip Larkin was born in Coventry in 1922. In that year his father was appointed City Treasurer, and in 1930 Larkin entered King Henry VIII School, which was a direct-grant grammar school. In 1940 he went to St John's College, Oxford, where he read English. This was early in the Second World War, and he was able to complete his degree (he took First Class Honours) in 1943, since he failed a medical for service in the armed forces. While at Oxford he became great friends with Kingsley Amis, who helped to shape his literary aims. Amis was to become an important novelist himself. Meanwhile Larkin left Oxford and took a job in a library in Wellington, Shropshire, a post he held for three years.

He began to publish occasional verse, and then a sequence of thirty poems in *The North Ship* (1945). In 1946 he published his first novel *Jill* and this was followed by another in 1947, *A Girl in Winter*. In 1950 he joined the library staff of Queen's University, Belfast, and in 1951 he published, at his own expense, *XX Poems*. Although this made little mark, in 1955 the Marvell Press published *The Less Deceived*, which included several poems from *XX Poems*. *The Less Deceived* made Larkin's initial reputation and established him as an important influence on other poets.

At about the same time he was appointed Librarian to the University of Hull, where he remained for the rest of his working life. Though his publications were sparse – *The Whitsun Weddings* did not appear until 1964 – Larkin's fame increased, and he was associated with the Movement Poets (such as Thom Gunn, Donald Davie and Kingsley Amis), who generally favoured direct expression, often commonplace, without ornamentation or obscure cultural references or any of the rhetoric which characterized the work of their predecessors (like the lush language of Dylan Thomas, for example). They were reasonable and for the most part could be easily understood. I give this brief appraisal of the Movement group above since they, in their turn, have been overtaken by literary change; I also give it because many of the phrases fit Larkin completely, and he is the one Movement poet who has survived the Movement.

His literary output has not been great. A student of jazz

throughout his life, he published a number of reviews in *All What Jazz* (1970). His next book of poems was *High Windows* (1974). He was awarded the Queen's Gold Medal for poetry in 1965, and was honoured by a number of universities. Throughout his life – he died in 1985 – he turned his back on publicity. He was a private man in a world which courts public display. His poems, one feels, embody his views, but it would be dangerous to read them as slabs of autobiography. He adopts voices and stances, tells stories, comments on society, fears death. He does not, like many poets of the twentieth century, load his verses with learning and reference so that his readers need to be cultured and cultivated in order to appreciate what he is saying. He admired poets as various as W. B. Yeats, Thomas Hardy, and Sir John Betjeman. He used symbolism sparingly, traditional forms innovatively; his language ranged from crude and explicit vulgarity, through cliché and colloquialism to mystical and visionary elevation. His poems are either short, very short or as long, occasionally, as two or three pages. They are conversational, confiding, lyrical, generally ironic, embodying repeated themes which will be examined in this commentary.

Do not read this as a cram book for A Level or GCSE; it is an invitation to an imaginative, sensitive experience, an aid to the appreciation of Larkin's work in the detail and in the mass. The individual reader will see much in Larkin which is not covered here, for this commentary too is an individual appraisal, describing and evaluating but aware that there may be other interpretations. Larkin brought to twentieth-century poetry an individual voice, sometimes voices, and he also brought a sharp awareness of his time; his style borrows and transforms, and his poetry speaks to a generality of readers rather than an intellectual élite. In short, he is a poet for all readers.

His techniques and themes are stressed in the following pages. He is a conscious artist, always aware of the form he is using, whether that usage is straightforward, experimental or innovative. Larkin has, I think, what great poets have in some degree, and that is to be particular, personal, but also to universalize the experience so that we recognize it as our own or grasp it emotionally, intellectually, as reasonable human experience. He is not a difficult poet, but he is a subtle one; he may say one thing and leave unsaid but imply another. His cynicism may conceal loneliness or sadness; a glib cliché may reflect a clichéd life empty of real language.

He had little time for scholars and critics who analysed his work, and would have deplored this commentary. But a private man becomes public property if he publishes poetry (or anything else, for that matter). And despite his modesty, Larkin is an important poet who has pointed English poetry in a particular direction. That direction will, I hope, become clear in the pages which follow. Remember that what is said here is commentary, and that the primary aim of this book is to send you to Larkin's poems and to enhance your appreciation of them.

This Study Aid is based on the text *Philip Larkin: Collected Poems* ed. Anthony Thwaite (The Marvell Press and Faber and Faber, 1988), but it can be used with any shorter collections (like paperback editions of *The Whitsun Weddings* and *High Windows*, for example, published by Faber and Faber). In order to provide a good range for the student, who can also see how Larkin's verse develops, I have included nine poems from *The Less Deceived* as well as the two editions referred to above. This gives a total of sixty-five poems and includes the most representative and important verse that he wrote. I give below a list of terms which are used throughout this commentary and which define or relate to techniques used by Larkin in his poetry.

# Literary terms used in these notes

**Irony and satire** Larkin is concerned to expose – to show the reader that what appears to be reality is not, that it is often insubstantial, illusory or even delusory. Life, or aspects of it, is a deception. Most of Larkin's attitudes involve the use of irony, for example in a poem like 'The Large Cool Store' where what is invitingly displayed constitutes a dream world which is not real – it is as fragile as the clothes themselves – or 'Sunny Prestatyn', where the desirable image of the girl on the poster is distorted and again represents a dream, not a reality. Larkin employs *satire* (the ridiculing of something which is a weakness, or of something morally wrong in the opinion of the writer). Larkin often parodies conduct, or attitudes, or the consumer society, including himself as middle-aged, as outsider, as anti-social (think of 'Vers de Société' or 'Annus Mirabilis' for example). As you read through the poems, you should be able to pick out those which are ironic or satirical, though sometimes both techniques are present, as in 'The Card-Players', where Larkin is being ironic about the realism of the Dutch painting and satirical in his use of caricature names for the players. Note also Larkin's choice of titles, which convey a great deal in themselves.

**Clichés, slang, etc** These, together with swearing, are often employed by Larkin: they are part of his ironic method, the commonplaces and platitudes which lack imagination and are used by him to deflate particular attitudes, situations, conventions. *Swearing*, like the opening of 'This Be The Verse', is a deliberate attempt to shock the reader into attention before exploring a particular theme.

**Themes** Themes which Larkin often uses are those of *loneliness and isolation*, often with himself as *outsider* (like 'Self's the Man' and 'Dockery and Son'). One of the strongest themes is that of *death*, his fear of it and its finality. *Personal relationships* also figure prominently; these are generally presented cynically and ironically, as in 'Talking in Bed', though there is very occasionally a conception of *love*, as in 'An Arundel Tomb'. 'The Whitsun Weddings', the title poem of the sequence, moves from cynical observation to an overall and expansive view of life at the end. The pathetic need for love is shown in 'Faith Healing'; one feels that Larkin's own need is best expressed in 'For Sidney Bechet' in the jazz musician's performance. As we have said earlier, Larkin probes *appearance* and *reality* with their corollaries *deception* and *truth*. He makes a number of insinuations about *the consumer society* (with *advertising* high up on his list of dislikes), and he is greatly concerned (this theme almost inevitably linked with *death*) with *time* and its effects and human *perspective*. Many of his themes deal with *failure*; and this is often connected with *self-deprecation* or mockery.

**Verse forms, rhyme schemes, imagery** Larkin uses a number of *forms* in his verse, and in the commentaries on individual poems which follow the form he uses – the verse or stanza, plus the rhyme scheme or the assonance or consonance – are indicated. *Assonance* is the repetition of vowels but not of consonants (sl*ow*ly and b*o*ny for example). *Consonance* is where the consonants rhyme at the end of words but not the vowels, (as in stro*ke* and lu*ck*). Among Larkin's forms are the *ballad* – often 4-line verses sometimes called *quatrains* – a suitably relaxed mode for him, since his poems, as a number of critics have noted, sometimes take the form of stories. *Metaphors* and *similes* abound, like 'the toad work' or 'like an arrow-shower'. Given the colloquial, conversational, relaxed tone of so many of the poems, Larkin is usually quite easy to understand. He employs *monologue*, rather like the dramatic soliloquy in a play, and varies this by what appears to be *dialogue* (though the answers are often silent, as in 'Mr Bleaney').

The best approach to a full understanding of his range and an enjoyment of his poetry (despite the morbidity of some of his themes) is to read the poems individually, respond to them as personal expressions, work out their techniques and themes, and note them down. In which of Larkin's poems do you find *humour*? Which of them share a similar theme? How does the form of the poem affect your appreciation and understanding of it? Ask yourself these and other questions as you read the poems and consult this commentary.

# Summaries, critical commentary, textual notes and revision questions
## Selection from *The Less Deceived* (1955)

(Extracts reprinted by permission of the Marvell Press Ltd)

### Wedding-Wind

The tone is relaxed and colloquial, though the movement of the verse seems to reflect, in its varying length of lines, the ebb and flow of the wind. The latter is at once outside fact and the symbol associated with happiness, the wedding-night consummation, the sense of security and of belonging. The woman is so happy that she is almost bemused by the outside elements, though her self-absorption is capable of opening up into compassion at the thought of the restless horses. There is a fine lyrical sweep in 'The happiness I had', a half-line which encapsulates her ecstasy. But there are curious emphases, like the use of 'he' rather than the intimacy of a name. Parts of the poem have this objective quality, yet we feel we are reading a small story. The last part of the poem expresses the wind as passion, as life force, with the rhetorical questions giving the experience a kind of spiritual, almost baptismal religious force. It is almost as if the force is creative – 'floods', 'new delighted lakes', 'all-generous waters' – so that even when death comes this experience and the recognition of it will remain. Spiritual language conveys sexual delight and discovery, with woman linked to nature in the totality of fulfilment. Perhaps this is best seen in the image of the beads which is both ornament and religious symbol (as in the rosary), while a phrase like 'bodying-forth' suggests birth. The kneeling cattle represent gratitude for what they are given, something which the narrator feels herself.

**ravelled** Tangled, frayed, here meaning that everything is out of place.
**bodying-forth** Giving shape and form to thoughts and feelings.
**all-generous waters** The phrase lifts the poem spiritually and has a
  Biblical association.

### At Grass

Five six-line verses, with conventional and consonant rhyme, beautifully descriptive, with a lyrical movement not dissimilar from the movement of the horses. The language is simple and sensitive (note the use of 'distresses' in line 3 and the 'seeming' of line 5 in the first verse). There is a good sense of contrast, 'anonymous' being picked up by 'their names were artificed' in verse two. The theme is of change, difference, age, the poet reaching out beyond the horses and making a comment on the nature of life. Verses two and three are a vivid evocation of the atmosphere of race and racecourse, with the final lines of the third verse capturing the final cheer of the crowd and transferring it to the fact of the result of the race in the paper. Verse four opens with fact and imagination ('memories' ... 'flies') and the brilliant suggestion of change and loss by the use of the positive 'all stole away', which carries the implication that they have been deserted. The further implication is that fame is temporary, unlasting, is forgotten in time. But there is also the suggestion that they have found a kind of peace away from the crowds, for the 'meadows' are 'unmolesting'. The irony deepens – 'their names live' – and the image of them having 'slipped their names' suggests that they have finally slipped their leashes – the training and racing that gave them fame is now no more. No one is interested; they are merely cared for with the minimum of attention. The poem is about the racehorses, but it is also a poignant poem, I think, about the nature of old age by analogy.

**To fable them** Unusual use of the noun as a verb, here meaning to celebrate their fame, to make them legends, with the poet perhaps being ironic about this.

**Cups and Stakes and Handicaps** Different types of horse-race.

**artificed . . . inlay-faded** i.e. inscribed on cups, silverware, maybe shields to show what they have won.

**classic Junes** The important races of the year – the classics of the sport – are run in June, for example the Derby.

**stop-press columns** Last minute news (of a race-result) inserted in the newspapers soon afterwards.

**Almanacked** i.e. the racing calendar which lists the records of the horses in detail.

# Wires

This is a good example of Larkin's sophisticated craftsmanship. It is a technically compact poem shut into eight lines, a trap between the first and last lines approximating to the situation of the cattle, enclosed, bred, slaughtered, a phrase like 'muscle-shredding' being both factual, fearful and anticipatory. Words are juxtaposed significantly (look at 'widest' and 'electric' in lines one and eight), and there is a neat abcddcba rhyme scheme which, reversing the first verse in the second, gives the effect of enclosure.

The broad theme of the poem is that we learn from experience to find our own limits. We have to conform, life is recognition and acceptance; we are all kept within the conventions imposed by society. There is a further implication that such restraint injures us, inhibits our fuller development or expression. The contemplation of animals with an accompanying analogy with humanity is seen in other Larkin poems, for example, 'Myxomatosis' and 'At Grass'.

**gives no quarter** Shows no mercy.

## Lines on a Young Lady's Photograph Album

Written in the relaxed colloquial style we have come to expect from Larkin, with nine 5-line verses, regular rhyme scheme of first and fourth line rhymes followed by second, third and fifth line rhymes (abbab). Verse one opens with sexual suggestions ('yielded . . . Once open') that distract the poet: this soon gives way to the 'sweets' images, with the album providing almost too much for him to digest. Each line in verse two is a picture of what the girl once was, while in verse three there is a faintly mocking – and self-mocking – tone, as if he is more suitable for her than the 'disquieting chaps who loll'. Then comes the comparison with art in the next two verses, with photography recording the actuality – it is dull, candid, accurate, it establishes 'a real girl in a real place'. But this leaves him to ponder – 'is it just *the past*?' This contemplation finds him greatly moved, for what was is all gone. In the seventh verse he comes to the conclusion that we are free to be moved by such things even if we were excluded from them, and there is no need to justify ourselves. Note that the poet has switched from the personal to the general, giving us a truth of human experience. In looking at photographs one can mourn (after all, nothing will happen): and the poet can even consider stealing 'one of you bathing'. The last verse offers a fine perspective on permanence in photographs no matter what happens in life, and single words establish the nostalgic and loving look back – 'calm', 'dry', 'heaven', 'lovely', 'Smaller and clearer'.

**furred** Fur trimmings on the hood of gowns worn by university
graduates.
**Hall's-Distemper boards** Advertisement hoardings for a brand of
paint.
**empirically** From the point of view of direct experience rather than
theory.


## I Remember, I Remember

This consists of seven five-line verses, ending with a single line
which has the effect of a climaxing couplet. The rhyme scheme
is deftly handled, a particular rhyme being picked up and carried over to the verse which follows, though not in a fixed order,
which gives the poem personal continuity and a conversational
rhythm. The conversational tone so typical of Larkin is
reinforced by another main strand of his technique – the use of
actual conversation (though sometimes you only hear one voice).
The natural ease of utterance comes at once, the visual picture
of arrival at Coventry (factually, Larkin's home town) accompanied by the edge of surprise. Typical too is Larkin's use of the
unusual word 'squinnied' and the commonplace irony of 'mine';
the latter conveys the personal and possessive flavour, the
security of our own identity and associations. At the beginning
of verse three the poet adopts his ironic fantasy voice: he is
deliberately mocking biographical detail which was thought to
be significant or sensational. The use of 'hols' is schoolboy slang,
an introduction to the sequence in his life of what didn't occur,
and the interpolation of his friend fails to move him from his
determined putting-down, exemplified in the negation 'unspent'
(Larkin is very fond of the negative as an emphasis). The next
three verses explore the sensational more fully. There was
nothing unusual, intellectually precocious, different in any way
about the poet and his experiences. He did not do what so many
claim to have done, either discovered themselves in outdoor
country life, or tasted youthful passion. He didn't even have his
early verses printed (with the implication that they were out-
standing), nor was his talent spotted: in other words, the autobiographical fodder supplied by authors when they look back (it
is conveniently coloured with hindsight) is deliberately withheld
by the poet – or perhaps it genuinely didn't exist. He is guying
the idea that such early details are of overriding importance

anyway. It is interesting the way his face is 'read' by his friend (misread is more accurate). 'Nothing' is revealed, either because in the poet's opinion there was nothing or because it was trivial; but we feel that the poet is perhaps playing games with the reader – he chooses not to tell what he thinks were the influences of his past on his present.

*I Remember, I Remember*  Opening line of a nostalgic, sentimental poem by the nineteenth-century poet Thomas Hood (1799–1845).

**squinnied**  Less common version of 'squinted', peered, looked out with eyes screwed up.

**cycle-crates**  Stands specially made to take the wheels of bicycles so that they can stand upright.

**Blinding theologies . . .**  Overpowering nature worship.

**an old hat**  i.e. something grotesque, unusual (did not happen).

**comic Ford**  Ramshackle old car.

**'all became a burning mist'**  A typical cliché used in romantic fiction to indicate passionate love.

**blunt ten-point**  A particular type-set used in printing.


## Born Yesterday

This colloquial poem is in two verses with a deftly constructed rhyme scheme: the tone is authentically Larkin, as is the content – that of the rejection of conventional sentiments (i.e. the 'fairy godmother-type gifts' to a new-born child) in favour of the wise but humdrum. As so often, the title carries some irony: 'I wasn't born yesterday' means 'I'm no fool', the implication being that only fools wish for what is exceptional in life. There is a visual quality in the first line which conveys the baby's screwed-up face, there is the relaxed and slangy 'Not the usual stuff' and 'lucky girl'. Half-rhymes contribute to the casual effect – 'bud', 'would', seen in the second verse too with 'balance' and 'talents'. The form is as perfect and complete as the baby itself, typical of Larkin's apparently effortless ability to bring content and structure into harmony: this is high art in verse. There are superbly emphatic single-word effects in the last few lines of the poem, where each word is a considered definition of a quality of life, of attitude or of personality. The theme is clear: beauty, or any extreme obsession or feeling or character trait, can make for the unbalanced personality which never achieves happiness. Consonance (note the 'l' sounds) is used tellingly in the second verse, while there is a daring paradox in the idea that being 'dull' makes for happiness. The overall effect is of sensitive, independent judgement, conversational rather than deliberately elevated, and this in itself is celebratory – of the child *and* of a new manner of unostentatious, direct, honest writing.

**Tightly-folded bud** New-born baby closely wrapped, but full of the promise of unfolding life, a 'blossoming'.
**skilled ...** Note the fine individual effects of these single words.


## Toads

One of Larkin's most celebrated poems, written in nine quatrains with alternate lines of consonance and with additional occasional rhyming sequences built in to it. The initial equation of the 'toad' with work is audacious, unexpected, outspoken. The implication is of something cold-blooded which dictates a pattern of existence. The tone is one of frustration and rebellion, the questions calling for a positive answer or rejection. The effect in verse one is immediate, while in verse two the bitterness of having to have such a commitment makes itself felt. In verse three Larkin begins to build up the idea of escape from work by citing examples of people, who 'live on their wits' – a range of con-men who survive. Note, as so often in Larkin, the choice of the unexpected in 'Losels, loblolly-men' balanced by the more acceptably anti-social 'louts'. The language generally is typical too – colloquial, fluent, even commonplace. In verse four there is the gypsy life as attraction, and this is continued in verse five. With verse six comes recognition of his own inability to rebel against the system, the coarse '*Stuff your pension!*' being balanced by a literary reference (reasonably unusual in Larkin). The last three verses acknowledge a kind of abject conformity within himself, so that he knows he will never be able to talk himself into achieving success – financial, personal, sexual – and that he is one of these grey ordinary people who must stay within the system. The last verse shows the nature of the compromise. You have work and escape from work, in other words leisure, freedom, imagination. One balances the other, may even lead to a fuller appreciation of the other. This is the compromise of all our lives.

**Losels** Worthless person, wastrel (archaic).

**loblolly-men** These were men who acted as medical orderlies on board ship in the British Navy in the eighteenth century.

**nippers** Slang for 'children'.

***Stuff your pension!*** Crude slang for 'you can keep your pension, I don't want it'.

**the stuff/That dreams are made on** A near-quotation from *The Tempest*, IV, 1, 156–7.

**hunkers** Scottish or northern dialect for 'haunches'.

**blarney** To flatter, to beguile with sweet talk, from the Irish tradition that kissing the Blarney Stone gives one the ability to charm with words.

**bodies** Gives body or shape to, fills out.


## Church Going

Seven verses of nine lines each with a regular rhyme scheme. Conversational tone, simple description for the reader, natural and easy establishing of empty church atmosphere. Note 'sprawlings', and the light irony used to register 'the holy end'. The silence is pervasive, and there is something slightly humorous in the removal of the cycle clips (the poem was written in 1954, when cycling would be popular, since many people could not then afford cars). His inquisitiveness is seen in the recording of details, and there is more humour when he assumes the role of the preacher by saying 'Here endeth' much too loudly for his own peace of mind. The donation of the Irish sixpence is funny too, but there follows, in more serious vein, his admission that he often visits churches despite feeling that this is a waste of time; which leads him to visions of the future, where their relics may be retained, or they themselves may be abandoned, or regarded as unlucky, since they are associated with death. The fourth verse takes him further – will churches become objects of superstition, supposedly able to provide remedies on the one hand or ghosts for the credulous on the other? He cunningly equates superstition and faith, but when each or both are gone we are merely left with physical desolation. This contemplation makes the fifth verse finely ironic, an examination and exposure of the various types of person who will be interested in churches in the future. The irony is directed at those who collect information and take pride in identifying it, the 'ruin-bibber' or the 'Christmas-addict', or someone like the poet himself who is drawn to it for what it tells of people – marriage, birth, and death, the records of humankind. There is an acknowledgement of a kind of faith, not Christianity but the faith of wishing to be associated with 'this accoutred frowsty barn', an unspiritual and frank description. He recognizes the 'compulsion' that it exercises over people, and sees change and the movement towards it as being important recognitions in individuals. The final line states what Larkin so often states in various voices, the irrevocability of death. Roger Day has rightly underlined the irony of the title, which can mean either visiting churches, or that the church is declining, or that they will be visited in the future. This embraces one of the favourite Larkin themes, the nature of time and its interconnectedness.

**sprawlings** Untidy straggling arrangements.
**Hectoring** Blustering, bullying.
**parchment** Valuable old manuscripts.
**pyx** Receptacle in which the host – the consecrated bread used during the communion service – is kept.
**simples** Plants, usually herbs, having medicinal properties.
**rood-lofts** Galleries on top of the rood-screen which itself divides the nave from the chancel. The galleries were used as access to the rood so that it could be cleaned and decorated.
**ruin-bibber** Ironic phrase, a bibber being a drinker, hence here someone addicted to ruins.
**gown-and-bands** Clerical gown and hanging white collar worn by priest.
**accoutred** Dressed, equipped with clothing.
**frowsty** Stale-smelling, musty.
**blent** Blended. This is an archaic word, like so many in the poem which sustain the atmosphere of antiquity, long tradition which is central to its theme.


## Myxomatosis

On the face of it, a simple eight-line poem with alternate lines rhyming. The fourth line is broken – as the rabbit is broken by the stick and by the disease. The effects of the disease are spelled out, for rabbits suffering from it cannot hear: thus 'soundless' is a superbly transferred epithet. The unvoiced question is qualified by 'seem', but the only practically humane answer to it is mercy killing. The poet's compassion is further underlined by the use of the word 'suppurate', for he is thinking of the terrible suffering in man-made traps as comparable to the blindness and distension caused by the disease. The last lines take up the analogy with people, for the instinct is to hope or pray for survival, for the fact that everything will 'come right again'. Larkin creates the atmosphere of death with colloquial, casual, sometimes understated phrases; he never falls into that bathos or caricature which so often occurs when animals are credited with thoughts or feelings.

**Myxomatosis** Severe virus disease of rabbits transmitted by mosquitoes – the eyes suppurate, the head is enlarged and full of sores, there is blindness and deafness as a result. In certain areas the virus was introduced to keep down the rabbit population.

## Revision questions on selection from *The Less Deceived*

**1** Which of these poems do you consider the happiest and why? Quote in support of your statements.

**2** Write about Larkin's attitude towards time in any two of these poems.

**3** By referring to two or three poems, show how Larkin is sympathetically involved with his subject.

**4** Consider the form of any two poems here, and show how it and the language influence your appreciation of the poems.

# Selection from *The Whitsun Weddings* (1964)

## Days

Ten short, unrhymed lines on the common Larkin theme of life and death. There is a staccato effect of statement and answer, or consideration, with a break after six lines, to indicate that the question does not admit of a reply. The short lines are as short and repetitious as days themselves. The echo of 'they' and 'days' conveys the monotony of work, the nature of daily existence. The break between the verses is ironic, with the suggestion that if we are to live on we must have faith and health. If we have the first we may believe what the priest tells us – presumably about the after life. The physical and spiritual attention is the focus of the last verse, with the final line suggesting space, freedom, to be cut short by death. The brevity of the poem is a comment on the brevity of life. The very simple language conveys the simple facts of life and death.

## For Sidney Bechet

Six three-line verses, generally with alternate lines rhyming, with a variant in the last two verses. New Orleans is the home of jazz. As in *Broadcast*, the mind's eye takes over, for 'appropriate falsehood' is the picture created by the sound of the music. This picture is of the jazz musicians and their 'Quarter' – a commune life of playing, dancing, making love, living idealized lives ('going shares'). The playing tells a story: there is a variety of pictures, of performances, of various listeners. But this gives way to the intensely personal, beautifully intimate reaction of the poet-listener. For him it is the consummation of loving and being loved in return. The Crescent City – New Orleans is often depicted with the moon shining over the water – becomes an everywhere which understands, appreciates fully, the 'speech' (music). The last two lines are something of a paradox – noise is equated with good – but it shows Larkin's ironic recognition that some would consider noise what he feels is the 'enormous yes' of existence, of love and loving. The last line shows Larkin's ability to effect a sudden change of mood. The 'long-haired grief' seems to be that of youth, 'scored pity' that of age, though 'scored' is a clever pun on 'music and 'marked'. The tone throughout is one of exhilaration, delight, even exaltation in the performer and his music.

**Sidney Bechet** (1897–1959) American jazz musician who played both soprano saxophone and clarinet.

**New Orleans** City on the Mississippi in Louisiana: an important port, it is renowned for its part in the evolution of traditional jazz.

**Quarter** Area of New Orleans known as the French Quarter, where most of the jazz musicians and performers were originally based.

**Mute glorious Storyvilles** A cunning combination, the first part of the phrase adapted from Thomas Gray's *Elegy in a Country Churchyard* (1751) where he writes 'Some mute *inglorious* Milton here may rest'. Larkin's 'mute' is an attachment to a brass instrument which softens the sound, glorious when used by Bechet. Storyville is a red light district in New Orleans named after a member of the US Navy who tried to close the brothels. It is also a present-day record label.

**Sporting-house** Brothel.

**priced/Far above rubies** Proverbs xxxi,10.

*manqués* Failed.

**plaids** Tartans (rugs).

**Crescent City** New Orleans.

**scored pity** Musical notation, the written form of a piece of music.

# Water

This is a beautiful lyrical poem in praise of water. The three verses are short, staccato, blank-verse statements. There is some irony, since religions already make use, and many have done throughout time, of water in ceremonial. The irony is at the expense of Christian practice, the emphasis here being on total immersion as purification. The implication is surely that water is the life force, and that it must be used completely and not just played with, dabbed out. It is the complete ceremonial symbol in itself. There is some passion in the poem, with 'A furious devout drench' perhaps mocking the civilized rituals of faith. The idea of water being the universalizing and transfiguring agent is seen in the last verse, the extra line carefully conveying the symbolic effect. The reference seems to suggest that religions should be universal, but the raising of the glass, and the permanence of reflected light, has the idea of there being a toast, a religious acceptance. It also recalls the raising of the chalice by the priest during Holy Communion. Water and the light reflected are radiant: the simple fact is celebrated as universal. Larkin, not religious or given to Christian observance, here conveys the essence of all religions, the consecration of the life symbol – water. The symbolism is evident; this is language loaded with associations and suggestions.

**fording** Crossing at the shallow part of a river.
**in the east** The altar is always at the east end of a church.

## Mr Bleaney

The form of this poem, as so often in Larkin, reflects sophisticated usage in an apparently casual and conversational mode. In factual terms, there are seven verses of four lines each – quatrains – with alternate lines rhyming. The form is that of the traditional ballad which tells a story. The story poem is a favourite Larkin device, and the story-line runs fluently from one verse into another. One technical aspect is the use of spoken words set against unspoken thoughts: this provides a fine, natural contrast. Larkin is exploring non-communication, for the unsaid words are themselves a silent commentary on what the landlady is saying. The poet captures her tone exactly. The pathos arises from the lonely life, both the poet's and Mr Bleaney's (though remember that the poet may be affecting his). The new lodger has points of contact with the old – and the 'one hired box' has ominous overtones of death, the death-in-life of this kind of existence, and the coffin.

The first verse points to the vulnerability of Mr Bleaney, moved from his job and then from his 'home', with the curtains a symbolic comment on the fragility of life. 'Tussocky' indicates the lack of care now that Bleaney has gone, while 'building land' expresses the threat of further urban expansion with its concomitant impersonality. Stark description at the end of the second verse merges into the fact that *he* is taking Mr Bleaney's place in the third. Typically Larkin are the slangy turns of phrase ('stub my fags'). Verse four is expressive of irritation, the noise of the radio, though 'jabbering' is perhaps descriptive of the landlady too, for she tells him all about Mr Bleaney's habits. These emphasize the pathos of Bleaney's existence – his trying to win money so that he can rise above all this, his holiday monotony (the poet has his full picture in the 'frame'). But he ponders on whether his own *thoughts* and *feelings* were common to Mr Bleaney, whether he accepted his way of life, realized that he was trapped, discovered nothing better in life, knew that he had to go on as he was. The throw-away fact that the poet doesn't know, can't know, heightens the pathos of loneliness, and establishes a kinship between him and Mr Bleaney: it is sad, muted, a blending of compassion and cynicism. The simplicity of the language echoes the simple and inescapable situation.

**the Bodies** The bodyworks section of a car factory.
**Tussocky** Full of clumps, dense tufts of grass.
**jabbering set** Radio always turned on.
**the four aways** One of the optional gambles on the weekly football-pool coupon.
**fusty** Smelling of damp, stale.

## The Importance of Elsewhere

Three four-line verses, with each verse having consonance in alternate lines. The poem is about recognition, accepting the fact that unfamiliarity, 'Strangeness', has its own attraction. There is a kind of 'welcome' in difference of speech (and culture), for each person recognizes the difference in the other — stranger views native and vice versa — and this makes for respect. In the second verse there is some fine description, a sense of perspective, with sights and sounds evoking the place, and this makes the writer feel that he is apart yet not disadvantaged, 'not unworkable' — he can adjust to the situation. He has the certainty that he will be accepted within it. He even feels, as the third verse makes clear, a sense of independence, an ability to stand up for himself which would not be acceptable in England. Here in Ireland, because there are no clogging conditions and conventions, a feeling of being watched and measured, he feels freer, and that his existence is not being undermined. This finality complements the form in the last verse, where full rhyme takes over from consonance.

**salt rebuff** Sharp snub or rejection.
**herring-hawker's cry** Fish-seller in the street crying out what he has for sale.

## Reference Back

Three verses, irregular in form: the first, six lines in rhyming couplets, followed by a nine-line verse with couplet rhymes, but running into the third verse of seven lines, the latter combining full rhyme and consonance. The theme relates to separation, even dissonance, in time and interest. The record is greeted with affectionate and clichéd response; the relationship, that of son and mother, marks their differences in age, in interests, in expectations. The second verse is a notation of the fact that the poet feels, after looking back to when he first began listening to records at home, that thirty years later he will think of the connection between them through this particular record. The key word in the poem is 'unsatisfactory'; they are only connected by being together at a moment in time rather than through anything else. He feels that we are not 'suited' to the looking back, because of what we have lost through moving on in time. Since time cannot stand still, when we look back we see how things have changed. We cannot keep past time intact.

**Oliver's *Riverside Blues*** Title of a piece by Joseph 'King' Oliver (1885–1938), American pioneer jazz cornettist.
**The flock of notes . . .** A very visual image of notes emerging like birds from the horns of the instruments played by elderly black jazzmen at a recording session.
**pre-electric horn** Old wind-up gramophone.

## Ignorance

The death theme is sounded again in this poem of three five-line verses, the first line of each standing on its own, the next four in rhyming couplets. The theme is our lack of knowledge in life and our capacity to qualify what we say, ending with our ignorance about why we die. The first verse is a parody of the cliché phrases (in italics) of ignorance. The second explains the various degrees of ignorance, of not fully grasping things, from the factual to the natural, while the third verse digs ever more deeply – we 'wear' (display) what we know, for this is the image we present in life, yet we don't know, particularly about death. The poem is also an exercise on our lack of precision, our tendency to qualify or fail to define and understand what we say and do.

## An Arundel Tomb

A poem having seven verses of six lines each and since, in a strange way, it is a poem of celebration, it has a lyrical tone. There is a regular rhyme scheme. The celebration is derived from the last verse, though the contemplation of the earl and countess seems optimistic. The observation is keen – 'proper habits' is the outline of their bodies and sculpted dress, while the idiosyncratic touch is the position of the 'little dogs'. The poet is initially concerned with the style – 'pre-baroque', which is plain – until he notices that the sculptor has modelled the pair holding hands. Perhaps it was done because, when they posed for him before death, they actually *were* holding hands, or maybe – while he was waiting for the long inscription to be carved – the inspiration for this intimate detail came to him. The fourth and fifth verses are remarkable in their compression and associations. The second line of the fourth has the fine paradox of 'stationary voyage', since they 'journey' through time but of course are tied to place in this effigy of death. The changes which are brought about by time are recorded: they are 'damaged' by the air, their tenants die in their turn, and new generations, unable to read the inscriptions, just look at them; there is snow, light reflects on the tomb, birds sing above them (note the associations of 'litter') and people visit the tomb. 'Washing' is good, since it is an attempt to decipher their identity. The second to the fourth lines of the sixth verse are a little obscure, though they perhaps record the manner of death in our own time, the smoke from crematoria as distinct from the physical representations on a tomb. The pair are 'untruth' because they are not like that in death, and were only 'momently' like it in life. The sculptor has been 'true' to what they were, but the simple idea of their love is preserved, and this is something we would wish preserved in them and in ourselves. It is symbolized in the empty gauntlet and in hand holding hand. *They* – and *we* – don't survive but their gesture, their attitude, symbolizes that what will survive is love, which transcends change.

**Arundel**  An attractive town in West Sussex which has an eleventh-century castle.
**proper habits**  Correct clothes.
**pre-baroque**  Before the heavily ornamented style of art and architecture which prevailed in the sixteenth – eighteenth centuries.

**gauntlet** Leather glove with large cuff.
**skeins** Literally a length of yarn or wool in a coil.
**blazon** Heraldic term meaning a coat of arms; also, a record of good
  qualities.

## First Sight

An exquisite lyric, two seven-line verses with a regular rhyme-
scheme. The poem symbolizes the changes in life, of the movement from one climate – emotional, experiential – to another.
The simple picture of winter birth, with the 'glare' off the snow,
is seen as 'unwelcome', lacking in comfort. The atmospheric
emphasis of cold is marked. There is observant detail in the
second verse ('wetly caked') and the promise of change, seen in
the wonderful conception of infinite surprise (which life yields).
The duality is seen in the idea of lambs being linked – though it
is unsaid – with humanity in terms of coming experience. The
beauty of the poem lies too in its Christian, religious associations.

## Love Songs in Age

As usual the form of the poem is worth noting; here three
eight-lined verses with regularly varying length of line which
gives a rhythmic effect, a lilt, with the climaxing couplet in each
verse equivalent to a kind of refrain.

The first verse focuses on the simple pleasures, a looking back
with the songs – music – as a permanent reminder of the past.
The third to the sixth lines record the commonplace happenings
over the years, but the seventh line personifies the songs as
having a life of their own, as indeed they have through their
sounds and their words, rather like poems. The first verse runs
into the second, the relaxed lines conveying the effect of chance,
but their rhythms perhaps making a sad music about this redis-
covered music. The poignant, pathetic note is struck when she
(the subject of the poem) goes back to when she was young. The
emphasis is on her having, then in that past, a rich future ahead
of her, a life of certainty, with implications of hope and
optimism. But the Larkin irony plays over the beginning of the
third verse with the 'much-mentioned brilliance', the theme of
so much music, love. Then for her it held the promise of making
everything come right; but life moved inexorably on and now,

'in age', she is forced to recognize that love had not done all that she had hoped from it then, and has achieved nothing for her now. The poem is a somewhat cynical appraisal of the nostalgic mood, the linking of the present with the past, the failure to achieve fulfilment in life.

**incipience** Starting to be, beginning to happen.

## The Whitsun Weddings

Eight ten-line verses with a regular rhyme scheme and rhythm which cleverly correspond to the rhythm of the train. The second line in each verse is shorter, almost to allow for the natural flow and pick-up of speed after a stop. This poem conveys the experiences of a particular journey: it depends for its effects on a relaxed flow, factual description, sudden arresting images, with the poet as observer recording the 'weddings' and the places they pass through. The opening of the poem is chatty and conversational, with the train leaving the town (Hull). The environs are indicated, with the last line of the first verse an exquisite description, an economic appraisal of perspective. From the train compartment we see a series of word-pictures. The poem is full of atmosphere (inner and outer heat), and the beginning of the journey is irradiated by flashes of imagination. The fine economy is evident in the second verse ('tall' heat for instance conveying its encompassing nature), with another series of word-pictures. Particularly evocative are 'stopping' and 'industrial froth' and 'short-shadowed'. There are combinations of nature and urban associations, as in 'acres of dismantled cars'. The first two verses are end-stopped, since this is factual description though imaginatively done. But since the evidence of the weddings is a kind of continuum from station to station, the verses begin to flow into one another. In the third the atmosphere changes: looking out on the sun the poet has ignored the shade – the covered platforms. The word-pictures continue to be vivid and economical ('parodies of fashion' – exaggerated imitations of what is supposed to be fashionable), but there is a light irony running through the descriptions from now on. Larkin's is a keen eye – he captures the momentary awkwardness of behaviour ('All posed irresolutely'). His curiosity engaged, the poet examines the groups, cramming in sight and sound pictures. He imagines the places where receptions (probably too grand a word) have been held. Particularly good is the focus on parents, fathers who have got their daughters off their hands and no longer have the expense of keeping them, while mothers are seen as sharing 'a happy funeral'. This is the sadness of losing their sons or daughters, with the happiness, the joy of the occasion, marriage. The 'religious wounding' is a reference to the wedding-night ritual of the bride losing her virginity to the groom. There follow more descriptions, accompanied by a cynical, low-key tone ('A dozen marriages got under way'). The factual reportage is of new lives together. In the seventh verse the irrevocable nature of what has been done is stressed. And gradually as the journey continues the poet begins to concentrate on his destination. The last line of this verse is a superb description in which nature (mail equals food for the mind) and the urban spread of London are connected. The main theme of the poem is found from the middle of the last verse onwards: the idea is of 'this frail ... coincidence' bringing together those who are married and who are beginning the experience of 'being changed' with the poet's contemplation of them and of life. These insights provide him with the idea of the poem as well as increased awareness. The final image, which conveys perfectly the sense of falling as the train begins to slow at the end of a journey, looks back to the opening line of the last verse ('aimed' ... 'arrow-shower') – the spreading of the marriages, their fertilization (sexual consummation) and the fertilization of the imagination which produces the poem. The ending is another example of Larkin's sudden and unexpected use of symbolism.

**skirls** Happy shouts, though the word is more commonly associated with the sound of bagpipes.
**pomaded** Hair slicked down with scented oil to make it sleek, shiny for the occasion.
**seamy** Lined.
**perms** Hair permanently waved.
**gouts** Jets.
**Odeon** Popular name at the time for a cinema.
**Pullmans** Luxury railway carriages named after their inventor, the American George Pullman (1831–97).

## Self's the Man

A stimulatingly ironic piece of light verse which consists of eight verses written in Larkin's favourite ballad form, though each verse has two rhyming couplets instead of the more common alternate line rhyme. There is a mixture of end-stopped and flow on verses. The main idea is of the poet being independent of marriage (though this may pathetically hide his own loneliness). The tone is slangy, the reader supposedly being addressed, while the appraisal of the marriage 'trap' is humorous.

Verse one shows marrying in order to prevent the chosen one marrying someone else, verse two satirically (and slangily) describes the responsibilities (children and goods), while the third shows the nagging, always-being-kept-occupied aspect of married life. The stance taken here and in verse four reflects the conventional, stereotyped nagging wife, downtrodden husband, and the mother-in-law who has to stay for a long period of time. From verse five onwards the poet compares his own life with Arnold's, and decides that each of them did what he did 'for his own ends'. This is what they thought would bring them most from life. The last verse asserts at first the poet's superiority – he feels that he knows what he finds acceptable (not married life, for instance) – but the last two lines reflect uncertainty. The idea of the van conveys doubt – mental breakdown, so that you have to be taken away – while the last line hinges on 'I suppose', a pathetic "I *think* I can cope". This is a deft, relaxed, self-ironic little poem. It develops a favourite Larkin theme, that of the loner, the outsider, the man who is his own man, but it ends with quizzical, self-mocking, self-recognition that 'self' may not be able to act independently.

**perk** Colloquial for perquisite, extra tip, addition to normal income.
**clobber** Slang word for clothes.
**sending a van** i.e. to take him to the asylum.

## Home is so Sad

Two five-line verses with alternate lines rhyming. As the title implies, the mood is sad, with the place and its objects supposedly experiencing the moods of change felt by people. The broken lines record absence, change, physical facts but something different in the atmosphere. Larkin is intent on the fact that homes (like people) start out to be something, to have ideals of achievement ('joyous shots') but fail to become more than a reflection of those who last lived in them.

The last two lines focus on the facts – the past, the things left still as they were. The home has seen the changes, the comings and goings. The poem is creatively sensitive to atmosphere, to permanence, absence, change. It is like a painting which records things but establishes at the same time their ambience, what they give to and take from their owners. It is therefore a comment on life.

## Afternoons

Three verses of eight lines each, unrhymed but consummately lyrical. The first verse is a word-picture, with 'hollows' (time scooped out) immediately effective. The appraisal here and in the second verse is of conventional lives, registered in the references to washing, the album, the television. In verse three there is a switch of emphasis to the way times have changed, the 'lovers are all in school' implying precocity, different standards from those of the past. Once more the poet is supposedly an outsider, observing, commenting, ironically evaluating. The observation is careful, noting increased urbanization. The last three lines register change more fully, since family responsibilities bring this about. There is increased weight, the lives of couples change as their children grow up, they no longer have independence but are diminished. Although the tone is mutedly cynical, the poem is a wise appraisal of what happens in life to so many of us. The poem is about young mothers at a particular time in the afternoon, but the theme is about change and the demands of parenthood.

## As Bad as a Mile

The title is an obvious reversal of the proverbial 'a miss is as good as a mile'. The idea of failure is registered in these two triplets of rhyme. It is almost as if a camera shot has been played backwards to show the apple intact and the action not undertaken. What is impressive is the progress from 'less to less' to 'more and more' to 'Earlier and earlier' which balances the negative, a favourite Larkin device, in the last verse. The superb economy of the poem conveys the immediacy of failure, lack of co-ordination. The implication is that when we act we often fail: perhaps it is better to just be still. But this itself is impossible.

**shied** Thrown.

## Faith Healing

Three ten-line verses with a regular rhyme scheme: as always the form is important, for the measured and flowing lines are a sophisticated equivalent to the measured and rehearsed utterances of the faith healer. The technical mastery runs throughout: notice, for example, that 'demands' in the American pronunciation would rhyme exactly with 'hands'. The first three lines are a straightforward description of the scene, with the healer almost anonymously delineated, the help of the stewards, then follows the sudden comfort in the image of 'warm spring rain'. We pause at the natural image – God blesses the earth, the rain provides natural sustenance and growth just as the healer in the name of God sustains hope. But the ironic tone of the poet is seen in the allocation of 'twenty seconds' only to each: 'scarcely pausing', 'goes into' and 'Directing' imply mechanical, ritualistic or even arrogant attitudes instead of humility. The final line of the first verse, running into the second, reflects the movement on from one batch to the next. The striking conjunction of 'exiled' and 'losing thoughts' shows how quickly each is forgotten after having received his or her allocation of blessing. This is contrasted with those who, greatly moved by the experience, respond emotionally to it. The image of the child, a frightening revelation of what may surface from deep within us, contrasts with the *'Dear child'* of the healer. The irony is deepened by the pathos of 'thinking' in verse two, for the theme of the poem is the personal need to be loved, hence the response here to the 'personal' quality of the healer. The unexpected use of 'blort' (see below) and the phrase 'jam and rejoice', a kind of contradiction, provides the key to the poem. This is found in the word 'love', repeated so often. The 'healing' is the expression of the need for love – they need to feel and receive and give. They think they have discovered it here, and the image of the thaw is a release of emotion in that recognition, which carries with it also the knowledge of what they might have been and what they might have done. The last half-line contains the hint at the truth, that this is all illusion. Larkin's compassion is ever-present after the middle of the second verse. Even the idea that the women themselves know that this is illusion but still clutch at it is seen sympathetically.

**Sheepishly stray ...** Isaiah liii,5: All we like sheep have gone astray ...
**blort** Bellow loudly, make a loud noise, cry.
**Moustached in flowered frocks** Elderly ladies with facial hair.

## MCMXIV

Four eight-lined verses of regular form, each with only the fourth and eighth line rhyming. The Roman numerals are perhaps deliberately used to record not only the year but the legions queuing up to fight. The poem, superbly controlled and perhaps referring to old photographs to convey the full atmosphere of the time, evokes the past in August 1914 at the beginning of the First World War. The men in verse one are those volunteering for the armed forces shortly to be at war with Germany, seen here just like crowds waiting to go in to a cricket or football match. The date is made clear in verse one, while verse two explores the period, for example when farthings (a quarter of an old penny) and sovereigns (gold coins worth an old pound) were in circulation as money. Further period references are shown in the names of the children, the advertisements, and the pubs 'Wide open all day' in the second verse, while the third renders the scene in the same period in the countryside. The pun on Domesday is effective, for the beginning of war sounded the Doomsday of a generation, while the fine line about the wheat shows the poet's detailed, sensitive observation. The limousines (early luxury cars) are also in period, but with the dust behind them in the then little-used roads. The last verse is direct, with the moving refrain line and its variant at beginning and end. These lines in particular show the poet's feeling that MCMXIV changed everything. It became the terrible experience that followed natural innocence. Marriages were broken by deaths and changed values in the years to come, and the old ways became the past 'without a word' (for many were silenced by death in the trenches). The poem is relaxed, colloquial, fluent, with the surface of the pictures of the past exposed and the terrible events and meaning beneath revealed and made explicit.

**The Oval** Surrey Cricket Club ground in South London. Test matches are played there regularly.
**Villa Park** Football ground in Birmingham, the home of Aston Villa.
**farthings** Old coins worth a quarter of an old penny.
**twist** A roll of tobacco.
**Domesday lines** Lines still faintly visible setting out the limits laid down in the survey of England carried out in 1086 and entered in the Domesday Book.
**limousines** Large luxury cars.

## Talking in Bed

Four verses of three lines each, with alternate lines loosely rhyming except in the last verse, where there is a rhyming triplet. There is light irony to begin with, which soon gives way to the problem of non-communication between those who through time and habit should find it easiest to communicate. The third line ironically suggests that since their marriage is based on being 'honest' it is strange that there is silence. The sudden switch to what is happening outside is effective because that 'unrest' contrasts with the silence within, and the perspective allows the imagination to work while the voice does not. What is conveyed is a sense of isolation (the poet's word at the end of the third verse). This is part of the irony which shows that they (the subjects of the poem) are together but cut off both from everything and verbally from each other. Once again the poet is reflecting on the limitations of physical intimacy. The last verse counterpoints 'honest' in the first, with the inability to be that now, what is left being the dishonesty of compromise or the outright break of wounding and hence arguing.

Particularly striking are the last two lines, which seem typical of Larkin's extraordinary succinctness and precision. To be 'not untrue and not unkind' is not to be positively true and kind, but is at least a compromise towards the higher human behaviour. It's a step nearer the ideal. It is a sad little poem.

**emblem** Visible sign of an inner truth.

## Take One Home for the Kiddies

Two verses of poignant description and commentary. The sing-song form, reminiscent of a nursery rhyme, pinpoints the irony. This is moral and social, and is relevant to Larkin's time and to our own time. The scene is the window of a pet shop: the animals are away from nature, are provided with the minimum ('shallow straw') and exposed to the glare from outside. Larkin here employs his own voice and that of a child. The two verses have alternate lines rhyming, the anonymous child – typical of all spoilt children – speaking in italics to convey the contrast in tone. In line three the negatives all add up to the terrible positive of the exploited situation.

The appraisal is another considered attack on the inhumanity of the consumer society. The habits of buying and providing 'things' for sale are evil, for here the creatures are as transient in their appeal as 'toys'. The last two lines sound another Larkin theme – that of death – but here it is ominous. The suggestion may be that the child (and his playmates) have killed, though perhaps inadvertently, the pet and are using it for their funeral 'game'. This gives the poem a sinister touch. It is an indictment of the way we live now, without concern for living creatures who only subserve our need, or the needs of our children, to be temporarily amused.

## A Study of Reading Habits

Three six-line verses with a regular rhyme scheme. It is collo-quial, slangy, uses swearing, in fact approximates to the fiction which provides the poet with his fantasies. The idea is of entering into what is read. It is an escape, we identify with hero (or villain) and we become strong, assertive, all those things which we are not in life. In the first verse a series of clichés ('dirty dogs', 'keep cool') sets the tone, followed in the second verse by fantasies of violence and sex, the 'inch-thick specs' disguising the evil and sadistic intentions and supposed actions. The poem is a parody of ghoulish fantasy. There is a witty pun on 'ripping', which is schoolboy slang for 'marvellous' and the factual ripping up of the victims. The schoolboy aspect is seen too in the comparison with meringues, both good to the taste and flesh and blood in colour. But the poet now affects to be grown up. Experience of life carries the penalty of finding out what you are really like – flashy and cowardly, never able to live up to the fantasy of your reading. This leads to cynicism: better to get drunk; books are not worth reading if you cannot be the monster or the hero and sustain the role in real life. The poem underlines, in its self-mocking stance, the way we like to think of ourselves and the way we are in reality.

**the old right hook** Boxing term for a right-handed punch.
**dirty dogs** bad characters, villains.
**dude** Dandy.
**yellow** Cowardly.
**stewed** Slang for 'drunk'.
**crap** Slang for rubbish.

## Ambulances

This is a poem in five verses of six lines each, completely regular in form, except that the first and the last (the latter naturally) are end-stopped. In each verse the first and last lines rhyme, with alternate lines rhyming in between. The poem opens with an arresting and unusual image which contrasts with the second line – the contrast being between that of enclosed silence and noise. The ominous note succeeds some straightforward description at the end of the last verse and the beginning of the second. Death and illness come to everybody. The repetitive 'they' gives 'them' an unobtrusive but firm personification – they are presences in our lives. To continue the image of the first line, they 'hear' the wounds of the flesh where the priest hears the wounds of the mind. The second verse describes the scene where someone is taken into an ambulance: 'momently' is a fine word to describe the speed, and 'stowed' – hidden away – conveys the inevitable impersonality of what happens. The third verse describes the immediate reactions of onlookers: the 'solving emptiness' is nothing, solved; an ironic glance, since only death is the final solution. This is what is 'so blank and true'. The emphasis on inevitability, so common in Larkin, is here pronounced. The last line in the third verse conveys pity for the person being taken, together with the recognition, inwardly at least, that one day it will be their turn. In the fourth verse 'sudden shut' has the atmosphere of being carried away from the past. This past fills the rest of the verse, where the person had an identity in the experience of life. In the last line here 'families and fashions' represents a fine contrast between the inner and outer lives, the emotions and the display. The break has come. The poignant isolation is the theme of the last verse. The second line is a moving recognition of severance from a loved one (or ones), while the idea of the 'room' moving through traffic shows the inviolable, cut-off nature of what has happened. The final two lines deal with the perspective of death, for this is close while all those connected with the life of the person are distant. It is typical of Larkin that he can concentrate on a daily occurrence in the urban scene and indicate its universality. And as always when the theme is associated with death, we sense the personal fear, or at least recognition, behind the poem.

**confessionals** The small compartments divided from the main body of the church in which a Roman Catholic priest hears confessions.
**plaque** The metal badge on the side of the ambulance which bears the arms of the city or county.
**cohered** i.e. connected, came together.


## Naturally the Foundation will Bear Your Expenses

This is a light, eight-line three verse ballad of supposedly personal narrative. The verses have alternate lines rhyming, and there is a lyrically ironic touch which runs throughout. Apart from the tone, the irony lies in the fact that he is leaving on Armistice Day, that he can traverse the world while leaving behind one which still mourns the dead of 'World' wars. There is a rejection of the 'Wreath-rubbish' at the Cenotaph, for the poet is intent on living in the present and not the past. The phrase 'solemn-sinister' perhaps carries the suggestion that it is wrong to devote ceremonial to the past, a sinister trait of the human mind to want to pay such tribute to death. But remember that the poet may be affecting a tone deliberately (this is one of Larkin's many voices), putting on an act, adopting the persona of the important travelling lecturer.

The verses are end-stopped. In the third verse Larkin uses slang to indicate contempt for the ceremonial, but the 'take off' means that he forgets the past and returns to the present. There follows a name-dropping sequence to underline how important he is in his present: the reference to Morgan Forster is interesting (the novelist who wrote *A Passage to India*). But this is a slick,

high-powered fast passage to India in which the present eliminates the past. It is easy on the tongue, sophisticated like the
supposed character who expresses it.

**Comet**  Large jet aeroplane.
**Berkeley**  University of California.
**Chatto**  The publisher Chatto and Windus, who might publish his book.
**the Third**  Radio Three, for whom he might give this lecture or another
talk.
**That day . . . Whitehall**  The Armistice Day service at the Cenotaph in
Whitehall on the Sunday nearest November 11th each year.
**throw up**  Vomit.
**Auster**  A poetic name for the south wind.
**Morgan Forster**  E. M. Forster (1879–1970), distinguished novelist and
critic.

## The Large Cool Store

Another ironic poem, dealing mainly with women's clothes,
what they reveal about people's tastes, and how they are conned
into buying. Alternate lines rhyme or half-rhyme in four regular
five-lined verses. The weekday/workday world is conjured in the
second verse, and this changes to a contemplation of synthetic
and glamorous nightwear on display. Then comes the pathos:
women who buy such garments are fantasizing, believing themselves to be something they are not. They are taken over by the
machine-made articles until they become machine-made in
response. They are lured into buying something different,
something away from nature and what is natural, something
'new'. The last lines emphasize this, but the final verse stresses
that men's wishes about them (women) may be unreal. Their
'ecstasies' are based on what they have acquired and what they
consequently think they are. They believe in their images, but
this has nothing to do with love.

**Hose**  Stockings.
**Modes For Night**  Nightdresses.
**Bri-Nylon Baby-Dolls and Shorties**  British nylon nightdresses
fashionable in the 1950s and 1960s.
**Flounce in clusters**  Displays of nightdresses, with the suggestions of
showing off.
**synthetic**  Artificial, here of fabrics but ironically of the consumer
society.

# Here

*Here* is Hull, one feels, where Larkin was the University Librarian. The four eight-lined verses run one into the other: there is a rhyme scheme which is varied cleverly, the first and third verses having the same, the second and fourth sharing the variant. The key word in the first verse is 'Swerving', which is repeated three times in order to define the name and nature of the place away from the main route to the industrial north. The movement of the verse corresponds to that of the train journey through the night. It is as always with Larkin, a series of compact descriptions, with workmen at one stop, then the countryside, and the estuary superbly delineated in detail, particularly the 'shining gull-marked mud'. The word 'surprise' in the second verse reflects the suddenness of discovery – the town is almost upon one without warning – and this is followed by the urban descriptions, the shopping scenes of the consumer society. The irony embraces this in all its goods-orientated superficiality. Yet the tone, though ironic, richly orchestrates the scenes through single-word or phrase effects: note in particular the last two lines of the second verse and the tolerance at the beginning of the third. Note too the use of 'terminate' and the unusual application of 'pastoral', the series of local word-pictures and then a fine run to the villages outside where, instead of urban monotony, there are individual dwellings and people. The last verse is evocative of that life outside, which seems to the poet to be infinitely preferable to the 'cut-price' lives he associates with the town. The 'here' of the first two and a half verses becomes the 'here' of nature, 'unfenced', 'untalkative', 'out of reach', negatives which are positives for the poet.

# Nothing To Be Said

Three unrhymed short verses with six lines to each. The cynical tone is again evident, and the theme is one of Larkin's favourites, the inevitability of death, for 'Life is slow dying'. It is the same whether you live in the primitive world or the urban crush of 'mill-towns'. The relaxed tone determines that whatever man does in his different ways, whether spiritual, sexual or commercial, spells out the slow movement towards death. Larkin uses contrast for effect, like that between 'hunting pig' or the refined 'holding a garden-party'. The last part encapsulates certain responses: to remind some people of what is happening does not mean anything to them (they just get on with their own concerns), while others have nothing to say about it anyway. Death comes to all: as so often with Larkin the flat or cynical tone is balanced by a compassionate overtone. Cynically, life is pointless since it is a movement towards death: realistically, people expend their energies making what they can of life before they die. There is, literally, nothing else to be said.

**nomads** Wandering tribes or peoples.
**cobble-close** living close together in the narrow cobbled streets.

## Broadcast

The three six-lined verses flow fluently into one another, cohere like the instruments of an orchestra as the poet listens to a concert on the radio (hence the title). In his mind's eye he creates the scene of the concert, the first verse evoking perfectly the sounds through associative usage, 'scuttle' and 'snivel' being particularly effective. Juxtaposed with this is the picture of a woman friend and her rapt response, followed by a gaunt and almost desolate picture of trees outside his window as he listens. 'Here it goes quickly dark' approximates to the lowering of the lights in the concert hall and the shutting out of the picture of her. The third verse describes the radio ('The glowing wavebands') and the effect the music has on him, reducing or neutralizing his imagination. The end of the poem (and of the concert) finds him trying to visualize her hands.

This is a poem of atmosphere, beautifully relaxed, smooth, its movements perhaps reflecting the movements of the music. It embodies a favourite Larkin theme, that of loneliness, but with imaginative connection and association with what is heard and inwardly seen. And, in a strange way, it is a kind of love poem. We feel that he treasures his mind's picture of the woman ('slightly-outmoded shoes' is endearing rather than sneering) and wishes he were part of her experience.

## Wild Oats

Light, perhaps fantasy verse with an ironic title (Larkin likes the proverbial starting points). The three verses have some rhyme but mainly consonance (for example 'worked' and 'sparked') in each of their eight lines. Here the poet casts himself in one of his favourite roles, that of the outsider who doesn't get the girl. There is the now commonplace slangy colloquial opening, conversational, flat, dated ('shooting-match' for instance). Simply, he fancies the beauty but goes out with the plain girl. The irony of the title is evident in the second verse, with the long engagement, later broken, the snatched meetings (probably dull and respectable – they were all in 'cathedral cities'), and shafts of wit ('unknown to the clergy'). There is also much typical self-mockery. The poet enjoys putting himself down, or so it seems, for he feels that 'beautiful' sees him as something of a joke. The 'rehearsals' is keenly ironic, descriptive of the attempts, botched like everything else, to break off the relationship. The stress is on being an outsider, failing to conform by doing what others do, perhaps just being not suitable for conformity. The fifth line of the last verse is a comic comment on what he has learned as a result, though it is doubtful if he could say exactly what that was. The 'snaps' (Larkin often uses the permanent index of photography) are 'unlucky charms' because they represent failure. But they are qualified by 'perhaps' – he thinks he's lucky that he didn't get caught, i.e. forced into marriage or a conventional life.

**sparked/The whole shooting-match off** Colloquial expression meaning to start everything off, to set events in motion.
**snaps** Photographs.

## Essential Beauty

This poem continues Larkin's criticism of modern society with its standards prescribed by urbanized advertising. Each of the two verses has sixteen lines and a sophisticated rhyme scheme: the lines are longer than usual in Larkin's verse, and maintain a kind of conversational rhetoric. The second but last line in each verse is shorter, facilitating an easy movement from first to second verse and then into the climactic statement of the poem. The main area is concerned with the advertising hoardings of great size, while the subjects mentioned – motor oil, salmon, butter, etc. – represent what people think they need and what they are conditioned to want. There is satire on the imitation of nature which characterizes so many adverts. All this is superficial, unreal, as is seen in the last line of the first verse which records reality. The delusory nature of the omnipresent advertising is fully spelled out in the second verse. The conjunction of 'crust', 'foam' and 'coldness' shows the perspective of variant purity: the real world, the poet suggests, is full of impurities called living. Advertisements invade the real world in their attempts to sell a kind of perfection ('essential beauty') which no one is capable of having or achieving. The real world is different, the pubs, for example, and the poet's own coinage of 'Granny Graveclothes' Tea', which is a parody of an advertising slogan. It suggests the immediacy of death which goes unadvertised. The 'dying smokers' may have a vision, just like an advertisement (wonderfully described in 'dappled', the play of light and shade), though it is of course a mirage ('As if on water'). Advertisements are like drinking, smoking, or playing tennis, an escape into dreams, or idealizations, or visions, before all is 'going dark' – the onset of death.

## Send No Money

There are three eight-line verses. Interestingly, the first four lines in each verse do not rhyme, the last four do. There is an unusual combination here of slangy cliché and direct, arresting, tightly compressed language. The brilliant personification of Time as a schoolmaster with a pocket watch gives way to the question about the truth of life and, to continue the image, the attempt to discover what it is that makes everything 'tick'. The use of 'lads' and 'bash' carries an overtone of young sexual activity. This is apparently 'unfair' from the poet's point of view, since what is and finding out what *really* is are different. The invitation of the second verse is simply a statement that experience takes over innocence ('green') and that it shapes life in so many ways. Experience *is* life, not definable in any complete form. The third verse cynically surveys the nature of experience. The writer sees himself, and perhaps others, as being injured by life, experiencing blows, but lustful, full of self, degraded by these experiences. He looks back on youth, finding out about life, which is itself as false as an advertisement. Since the truss is a support for the male genitals, the sexual implications of the poem are evident. The title deliberately omits the advertiser's usual accompaniment – 'Send No Money: Satisfaction Guaranteed'. The poem is an ironic commentary, as so often in Larkin, on life: and to use his own word from 'Reference Back', its experiences have been 'unsatisfactory'.

**fobbed** The image is of the fob, a watch pocket in the waistcoat, or the chain attached to a pocket watch.

**Impendent** Unusual use of the verb 'impend' – to hang or depend – conveying a sense of pomposity or gravity.

**itching to have a bash** Colloquialism for very keen to have a go, do or learn something new.

*There's no green in your eye* A slang expression meaning innocence, immaturity, being easily led, hence here the reverse of those.

*clobber* Beat or batter.

**visor** Literally a piece of armour attached to the helmet to protect the face – also a mask or disguise.

**Sod all** Vulgar expression meaning 'nothing'.

**Truss-advertisement** A surgical support for a hernia, hence an object of ridicule or scorn, here ironic and derogatory.

## Toads Revisited

A favourite Larkin theme (how to occupy yourself before death carries you off), this poem should be read in conjunction with *Toads*. It has the same laconic throw-away tone which characterizes Larkin at his best. The consonant rhyming runs throughout the poem, which consists of nine four-line verses in couplets. The tone is conversational, relaxed, colloquial, even confiding, easy to understand. The poet's stance is clear by the end of the second verse: having time to kill does not fit in with his temperament. The low-key verses are themselves a comment on a kind of leisured, low-key life. Larkin captures the various wandering-around-the-park experiences vividly. He sees youth and age, the 'out-patients' and the tramps, and refers to his earlier metaphor for work (the 'toad'), while criticizing those who are 'stupid or weak' by dodging work. His repetition of the exclamatory line ('Think of being them') shows how much he despises – but really fears – having time on his hands. The simple phrases are emblematic of the simplicity, which is the reality, of this kind of existence. There is too much time to brood (verse seven) and nowhere to go but 'indoors': to leave home and return to it is part of the daily ritual of trying to use up time. The last two lines reflect a decisive – though perhaps temporary – swing: the way to delay death, or thoughts of death, is to work. In the last verse there is a symbolic effect too. By four o'clock it is dark, and darkness (which symbolizes death) has to be lit artificially so that one may work on. Work is finally seen as something that keeps you going as you get older. Pathos, fear, and a wry humour, are apparent throughout the poem.

**Palsied** A form of paralysis, usually with involuntary tremors and jerks.
**Hare-eyes** Suggesting madness, as in Mad March Hares.
**jitters** Nerves, jerkiness.
**lobelias** Small, bright blue flowers.
**loaf-haired** Hair-style fashion of the 1960s. The hair was back-combed to make it stand up high, and heavily lacquered to hold it in place.

## Sunny Prestatyn

Three eight-line verses, with the rhyme scheme and half-rhymes cunningly varied. The initial focus is on advertising and the crude appeal, through sexual invitation, to the consumer society. This lure is balanced by an important comment on the ephemeral nature of existence, its fragility and vulnerability, while the poster becomes a symbol of defacement and degradation. The artificial girl, as artificial as the society she is exposed to cater for, is despoiled like that society by its sexual lusts. Advertisers expose and man, in the shape of Titch Thomas, disposes his crude satire. The desecration of the poster equals the desecration of man. The jokes are evidence of sickness – the adding of the moustache, the violence, the sexual indulgence and obscenity. The slangy language ('Huge tits') is part of the larger than life advertisement which invites larger than life comment, which it gets from the defacers of the poster. If this interference is a disease of society then the disease in the last verse is captured in the last line. *'Fight Cancer'* invites no desecration, since it is itself a desecration of life. The description is inlaid with the Larkin irony at the expense of advertising, of life, of obscenity, of man's tendencies and fantasies (the poster girl is a fantasy). These are punctured by reality. The language is colloquial, slangy, descriptive, visual (like the poster), cheap and nasty (like the poster). There is a varied length of line and some emotive usage (like that of 'hunk', which the males looking at the poster might wishfully apply to themselves). The climaxing line, as I have said, makes the replacement poster a comment on the cancerous mutilation of the original.

**slapped up** Refers to the action of the bill-poster who literally slaps the large sections of advertising sheets on to the hoarding with a long brush.

**snaggle-toothed and boss-eyed** Defaced by vandals, with some of her teeth blacked in and her eyes made to look in different directions.

**fissured crotch** The vandals have emphasised her genitals – distorted into a long narrow crack.

**tuberous** Swelling, fleshy, as a plant tuber.

**cock and balls** Vulgar reference to the male genitals.

## Dockery and Son

There are six eight-line verses, alternate lines rhyming in the first and variants thereafter. The poem captures and extends something we all experience, a return to the past which carries the inevitable recognition of change. The poem opens with a question, the inward balancing the outward as the past is recalled and the information '"His son's here now"' is digested. Note 'Death-suited', perhaps implying that the narrator has come back to college for a funeral, while 'visitant' has a supernatural association, as if he is a ghost come back to haunt the past. The banal conversation yields to memories, like being summoned to the Dean for explanation of behaviour. The verse ends cleverly with the attempt to open the door: it symbolizes the past which we cannot re-enter. Short sentences convey the reflex happenings before the pathos of anonymous departure: a sense of loneliness pervades the poem. Note the favourite Larkin device of having one speaker followed by the silent listening companion. There are staccato half-lines in verse two, expressive of fragmented passing experience. The heavy alliteration of the 'c's' in this verse emphasizes the finality of the goodbye; by the middle we are well into the consciousness of reminiscence. This may be autobiographical (Larkin would be about the same age as the narrator), and there is speculation about, perhaps envy of, Dockery's young fatherhood. Once again the fragments of life, of life's journey (symbolized by the train journey here) are captured, even down to the 'awful pie' – the irony being that he has had to swallow more than this. The pondering suggests how little we know about others. The run on into the fourth verse has the beautifully poetic 'unhindered moon' (symbol of love the poet hasn't experienced). There are reflections on marriage and responsibility as well as those on the passage of time. In this verse too there is a sense of separation, of difference and isolation. The question he is posing to himself is whether Dockery knew what he wanted and got it, even to the certainty of knowing he wanted a son. The last two verses become more rational, with the idea that for him (the poet) 'increase' would mean 'dilution' – marrying and having children would be a lessening of self. This thinking leads him to feel that 'Innate assumptions' (like the need to get married) don't come from what we believe to be right or what we 'want to do', but are rather a convention, which takes on the form of a habit, and then becomes all that we possess and live for. This is typical Larkin analysis – they provide Dockery and his kind with their reason for existence, whereas for the poet they are as nothing. The last four lines emphasize Larkin's attitude towards life – it is habit, ignorance of others, and finally death. The poem conveys the experience of the visit, the influence of the past, the journey back with its reflections, and then the considered analysis of life and its conventions, our differences from others and finally, and fittingly at the end of the poem, death, always the oppressive finality for Larkin.

## Revision questions on *The Whitsun Weddings*

**1** Write a full appreciation of either 'The Whitsun Weddings' or 'Dockery and Son', showing Larkin's main techniques in one of his longer poems.

**2** Compare and contrast any two poems in this sequence.

**3** Show how Larkin treats the theme of death in any three poems.

**4** What aspects of society does Larkin dislike most? You should confine your answer to any three poems.

**5** Show how Larkin uses either cliché or monologue in any two poems.

**6** Write about any two poems here which seem to reflect an optimistic attitude towards life or an aspect of life.

**7** Larkin uses irony in a number of poems. Select two or three from *The Whitsun Weddings* and bring out the quality of Larkin's ironic presentation.

**8** What do you consider to be the most important theme in any three of these poems and why?

**9** Write about Larkin's use of symbolism in any two or three poems.

**10** Which of Larkin's poems do you find humorous and why? You may refer to two or three in your answer.

# Selection from *High Windows* (1974)

## Solar

Slight but attractive three-verse poem about the sun, written in short but expressive lines of free verse. Larkin's descriptive powers are economically evident, the first line and the use of the word 'spilling' in the second registering at once. Superbly effective too is the word 'unfurnished', which describes the vast spaces around. The poet sees the sun as a flower, standing stalkless, with its 'petalled head' 'unclosing' as undemandingly and generously as a wild flower. The final line of the first verse conveys the completeness of the sun's giving. Note how the sun is heard as well as seen ('exploding', 'echo'), which emphasizes its power. The 'Gold' of verse two leads naturally to the 'Coined' of three, this last verse reflecting the movement of the sun from the horizon ('Lonely horizontals') through the measurements of time (the sundial). The fifth line suggests that man's moods and expectations are measured by time – we are elated or sustained by the constant giving (warmth) and by the permanence of its presence.

## How Distant

As the title suggests, this is a poem about perspective. Five verses with alternate lines rhyming in the second and fourth, the first and third unrhymed. The theme is of the young, leaving home, exploring, discovering, with a series of word-pictures picked out clearly and sometimes unusually by the poet. Dated references include those to the cordage (ropes of the rigging) and the 'Melodeons' (small reed organs) which convey the sense of the past (How Distant) when people sought escape and adventure. The picture of the girl conveys the cramped conditions of the boats in the past, what you had to endure in order to achieve. The comparison in the last verse is unusual – it is between the clothes turned out by great numbers and those whose great numbers established new places. The sense of the last verse is highly condensed. The tone throughout the poem is typical of Larkin and, as well as the unusual words, we find double-barrelled epithets like 'salt-white' and 'differently-swung'.

**steerage** The cheapest accommodation on a passenger ship.
**Ramifies** Develops, becomes complex – here meaning that imagination
can run riot, make fantasies (about the girl).


## Friday Night in the Royal Station Hotel

Written in the form of a sonnet, but Larkin has nine lines in
what would normally be an octave, and five in the sestet. The
theme is loneliness throughout, but particularly in the first section where alternate lines rhyme. The furniture is alone with
itself, the hotel's guests have departed. The sense of atmosphere
is finely done, the image in the sixth line 'And silence laid like
carpet' capturing place succinctly. The broken lines reflect the
weekend break itself, and the last five lines convey the sense of
isolation, loneliness, with pathos, the bracketed ('If home exis-
ted') expressing that exactly. The italics of the final statements
indicate the closing in of night both here and in homes beyond.
But the preceding word is 'exile', once again evocative of the
atmosphere in the hotel.

**shoeless corridors** Another fine use of the negative by Larkin – there
are no guests to leave shoes outside bedroom doors for cleaning.


## High Windows

Five verses written in quatrains, with the outspoken and blunt
opening setting the tone for the early part of the poem which
leads to a contemplative retrospect on being young, enjoying
oneself without responsibility, and not being tied to convention.
Larkin often sets out to shock, though nowhere more effectively
than here, dated though the sexuality of the first three lines is.
The theme of the poem is the change from youth to age, with
the concentration on what it was like to be young. The poet
conjures the perspective of youth and that of age, and with a
typically self-mocking note thinks of himself young, with the
idea of living for pleasure, rejecting God, not thinking of sin and
moral pressures. The time of youth is that of rebellion and
rejection, but as he thinks back to it he is overtaken by another
vision. Words are not enough to describe it, rather it is an image,
a mystical experience which evokes freedom and space away
from the constraints of life – and youth – and their particular
escapes. The directness and crudity are replaced by a conception

that is beautiful, the idea of infinity which goes on for ever. The tone of the poem has changed from the colloquial to the poetic. The ending is symbolic of freedom, though it may come from the fact, as Roger Day has pointed out, that Larkin was responsible for the building of an extension to the library at Hull which has windows set high up on the walls. They are a noteworthy feature.

**long slide** Happy childhood days in the playground are invoked but evocative of early sexual experiences as well. The theme of freedom from restraint is expressed here.

**high windows** Symbolic of a greater freedom, from convention, and perhaps spiritual and far-reaching.

**sun-comprehending glass** Wonderful idea of freedom being all-pervasive. A symbolic ending.

## The Trees

This beautifully observed poem is in three quatrains which have the first and fourth lines in each rhyming, with a rhyming couplet sandwiched in between. The lyric is about life and death, but it is the poignancy of the conception that is so moving. The poet sees in the buds 'a kind of grief', perhaps for the previous year's blossom or at the thought of their own 'death' in the coming year. Noteworthy is the sound of the poem, an echo in its crisp and simple words of the compact completeness of each bud. The second verse is consummately crafted, and again the sound, particularly of the last line, is a lyrical celebration (despite the death image) of the cycle of nature. The opening of the third verse is vivid and unusual, with trees compared to castles (the branches, spread, are their annual full fortification); the image suggests power, the overcoming of the past death in the richness of full birth. This is Larkin at his best in the sense of fine, economical descriptive power and the accompanying focus which gives the trees a symbolic quality.

**written down in rings of grain** The rings formed in the trunks within their grain, a means of calculating the tree's age.

**thresh** Movement, strength, with harvest associations which have a feeling of rich fertility, new growth.

## Annus Mirabilis

A short slangy poem, four verses of five lines each, with regular rhyme scheme. The opening is intent on shocking. Larkin has ironically taken the title from Dryden's poem of 1667, the 'Year of Wonders', which saw the Dutch fleet defeated by the English fleet as well as The Great Fire of London. Here, in Larkin's poem, supposed personal history takes the place of major national events, though the cultural events of verse one are important. In 1960 Penguin Books defended their right to publish the unexpurgated version of D. H. Lawrence's *Lady Chatterley's Lover* and won. The pop group The Beatles broke through into a best-selling category, the like of which had never been seen before. The self-mocking 'rather late for me' (Larkin would be forty-one in that year) shows a familiar irony of stance. The second verse records the past, where marriage was still the major convention and sex was still regarded 'A shame'. Verse three is satirical about the supposed liberation, particularly sexual, that was initiated by the events of the first verse; Larkin uses clichés ('breaking of the bank', a 'game') to underline his own sarcasm at what actually happened. The last verse, like the refrain of a song, repeats ironically the main lines, with a significant variant in the first. Larkin is laughing at himself and at the idea that the Swinging Sixties constituted any real freedom or progress.

**A wrangle for a ring** i.e. the engagement ring which girls in the pre-permissive society regarded as the pledge that the man would stand by them if they became pregnant.
**breaking of the bank** Cliché expressive here of sexual freedom and indulgence.

## Sympathy in White Major

Here three eight-line verses, self-mocking and sad in parts, in which the poet affects to drink to himself. The first verse makes clear just how stiff the drink is. The 'Sympathy' of the title derives from the French poet Théophile Gautier's 'Symphonie en blanc majeur', Larkin having deftly changed the word to fit himself. While the meaning of the first verse is clear, that of the second is a little obscure. Larkin has condensed here the effects of his supposed living for others, though his cynical appraisal leads him to think that for him and for them it was a form of delusion – common delusion, he is suggesting. The third verse, deliberately italicized with the exception of the last line, strings together the clichés which will perhaps be uttered of him after his death or which are uttered after any death; it is a scathing indictment of the stereotyped and insincere tributes which are paid and which are meaningless. The sting of the last line is emphatic; all praise of such decency is meaningless, since it is praising something you don't really like. In a brilliantly condensed piece of symbolism Larkin has given us a profound truth: he has defined the name and nature of hypocrisy.

**Three goes** i.e. measures.
*Straight as a die* Totally honest. Die is the singular form of dice.
*A brick* Someone straightforward and dependable.
*a trump* A fine reliable person (from the suit chosen as trumps at cards – a winner).
*the whitest man* The best, most decent person (a compliment).


## Sad Steps

The starting point is Sir Philip Sidney's sixteenth-century love sonnet which begins:

With how sad steps, O moon, thou climb'st the skies,
How silently, and with how wan a face.

Larkin's tone is a deliberate debunking of romance. The relaxed realism of the colloquial opening soon becomes contemplative and finely descriptive at the same time. The movement of the clouds, the 'cleanliness' of the moon, are described with fine observation, a word-and-atmospheric picture. But in the second verse there is self-mockery as well as fine description. The third is the picture filled in and with movement. The symbols of the moon in its classical associations and the myths associated with it are stressed in the fourth verse, and the fear (wolves, the supernatural) is carried into the fifth. All the pain and suffering deriving from love is spelled out in the final verse, a looking back on the wounds of love and the knowledge that although we cannot suffer in the same way again, someone, somewhere, *is* suffering. As so often with Larkin the unusual word arrests the reader's attention, here 'Immensements!' Note that each pair of triplets has a regular rhyme scheme. Interesting, and musical, are the number of words ending in -ss.

**Sad Steps** See above, but sad steps also for the poet having to leave the landscape and go back to bed, and also further steps away from his lost youth.

**thick curtains** Factual, but metaphorically those between youth and age too.

**Lozenge** Sweet symbolizing love.

**Medallion** This implies a decoration or award. The moon is a permanent inspiration to artists in words, in music, in painting.

**Immensements!** A coinage, the implication being the enormous idea of passions recalled.

## Posterity

Original and funny poem in which the writer affects to have a picture of his biographer and the latter's attitude towards him. There are three verses, with the first and last lines in each rhyming (roughly), while inside the frame alternate lines rhyme. It is a piece of imaginative whimsy, an ironic view of the supposed biographer being trapped inside the research he is compelled to do on 'this old fart'. He has a cynical attitude towards his subject and no sense of affinity with it. He is only doing it so that he can get the credit for it, either by publishing (putting it 'on the skids') or being awarded a higher degree for it. In fact the biographer feels contempt for the subject, who was *'natural'* and 'fouled up'. The language as so often is colloquial, here Americanized; there is a further irony in an English writer being written about by an American. The latter would much rather be working on something stimulating like 'Protest Theater'. The poem is a send-up of academic research, viewed cynically as a means to an end and a way of passing the time without much responsibility. The language, with swear words and clichés, reflects the lack of interest and self-discipline.

**sneakers** Plimsolls or training shoes.

**tenure** Job security.

**this old fart** i.e. the subject of the biography, the poet himself.

**on the skids** Get rid of it (maybe publish it).

**semesters** Terms.

**Protest Theater** i.e. productions against the establishment, involvement in war, etc.

**Freshman Psych** Pompous writing found in psychology textbooks read by first year American university students.
**fouled-up** Confused, muddled.

## Homage to a Government

Three six-line verses, with a repetition of particular words as rhyme instead of other eye or sound rhymes. It establishes a flatness, perhaps equivalent to the simple flatness of the decision. The title is a sarcastic one, since a moral stance is taken up in the poem about the decision through the running irony. Inevitably there is monotony because of the repetition, but the language reflects received comment and explanation which are inadequate and convey a disturbing degree of apathy. The second verse probes the decision and registers the apathy with which it is received. The third verse, employing the same repetitions, is brusquely cynical – we have lost integrity, we have saved money, which is now all we have. The theme, true in its emphasis, is that political decisions are taken for reasons of expediency, that there is no such thing as national or moral responsibility. The innuendo is of betrayal which will soon be forgotten or absorbed. Governments rule by economics not morality. The style mentioned at the beginning underlines this statement's appraisal of debasement.

## To the Sea

The form is of four nine-line verses with a regular rhyme or/and half-rhyme scheme. The first verse is a superb evocation of memory into a word-picture; tone relaxed, conversational, the simple language of retrospect. There is the unusual and effective use of 'miniature', the mixtures and crowdedness seen from a distant perspective. But the poem is set in the present too, as seen from the second verse ('transistors'); there is contrast between the treatment of youth and age, the note of pathos sounded in the last lines of the second verse. The third verse is unusual Larkin in that it has what appears to be biographical recall of his own seaside holidays – searching for cigarette cards ('Famous Cricketers') and remembering 'the same seaside quack' (a fine capture of passing sound) as his parents had done. In these last two verses there is an insistent sequence of word-pictures which I feel would be familiar to many of us. The best lines of all describe the change in the texture of the sunlight. What has earlier been described as a 'ritual' (the holiday by the seaside) is spelled out yet again. It is not cynical but realistic in its appraisal, childhood and age again connected in happiness and responsibility.

**uncertain children** Unfamiliar with the beach.
**The rigid old** Rigid now, from rheumatism or arthritis, all too soon to be rigid in death.
**Famous Cricketers** Cigarette cards in packets, free with each one, in various series.
**quack** Fake (perhaps someone selling something or offering cures).


## The Explosion

The subject is a mining disaster, the treatment is a compound of time shifts and vivid actuality. There are eight verses – triplets – unrhymed but emphatic, with one final extra line eternalizing the moment of the explosion through the arrested day, symbolic of the span of life. In fact there is a marked degree of symbolism in the poem. In the first verse note the combination of hard sounds and alliterative 's' sounds, as well as the 'shadows' which are an unobtrusive forecast of what is to come. In verse two there is the fine 'oath-edged', and the effect of the silence, another contrast with what is to come. The simplicity and pathos balance each other in verse three, with the eggs stored for a later retrieval which never comes. The fourth verse, with its single-word effects, picks up a kind of *Hiawatha* rhythm to convey the movement, with the word 'passed' a euphemism for their coming death. The outward effects comprise verse five, while in the sixth the poet cuts into a quotation from a service for the dead. The explosion as such is by-passed; the effect is everything. The reference to 'chapels' confirms the Welsh location of the poem, and just as religion evokes a vision, so here the immediacy of the men 'Larger than in life' enters the imagination of their loved ones. The climactic line has already been referred to; it shows a perspective, a condensed appraisal of what has happened and what remains.

**moleskins** Trousers made from the hard-wearing fabric of cotton, and thus suitable for working clothes.

***The dead go on before us*** ... 'In my Father's house are many mansions. I go to prepare a place for you.' John xiv,2.

## The Card-Players

Unusual form, in that it is nominally a sonnet – fourteen lines, but the last line is deliberately dislocated from the others, though it rhymes loosely with 'trees'. The form underlines the irony, since sonnets are usually on romantic and elevated themes. It is a brilliant verbal evocation of a Dutch painting, the language giving particular clues about the period. But since the painting so to speak is already done, the poet animates it by imagining movement and sound, and deliberately coarsens the experience by giving the characters crude names and actions. In other words, he is writing his own earthy drama for the visual equivalent. Earthy actions accompany this, pissing (lines 1–2), drinking and smoking (4–6). Snoring and singing are the next sound effects. But even the low-life scene has poetic elements, as we see in the fine description of the 'century-wide trees'. There is the usual attempt to shock – successful I think – the life behind art being crudely revealed. We have a feeling that Larkin delights in confronting the reader with this animalistic level. The last line is masterly. The outside ('Rain, wind and fire!') has its equivalent inside, with the pissing, belching, farting, snoring, gobbing, a natural ('bestial') equivalent to the sounds of nature.

**The Card-Players** The title of a painting by Teniers the Younger (1610–90), though there is another called 'Card-Players in a Tavern' by Adriaen Brouwer (1605–38).

**clay** A clay pipe.

**ham-hung rafters** Pigs were killed for food, the hams being hung over an open fire to be smoked and thus preserved.

**the queen of hearts** Perhaps the card in the pack, but if it is the Teniers picture it may be Larkin's cruelly ironic description of the crone sitting by the fireside.

## Dublinesque

This moving short lyrical poem (despite the initial subject) has a beautifully sustained use of consonance: there is no formal rhyme but the brisk lines are resonant with a kind of music. In the first of the six-line verses the scene is set, with direct and immediately arresting observation ('light is pewter') and finely selective contrast ('race-guides and rosaries') which span the lives of so many, in religion and gambling. With the mention of the funeral we expect a Larkin treatment of death, but the main emphasis is on the prostitutes and their somewhat grotesque actions. It is a vivid picture, almost a celebration or street wake, but the note of sadness is struck in the final verse. The fact that the poet doesn't know whose death it is comes to mean that it is 'All love, all beauty', that the song is for all those who are loved. The poignancy is in the universality, the 'What will survive of us is love' theme which answers those who assert that Larkin is merely cynical. The moment he has captured is one of beauty because of the simple, natural, unselfconscious expression of love.

**stucco**  Cement or plaster coating for outside walls.
**rosaries**  Strings of beads used for praying in the Roman Catholic church.
**streetwalkers**  Prostitutes.
**Leg-of-mutton sleeves**  Large puffed shoulders narrowing from the elbow into sleeves tight to the wrist.

## This Be The Verse

Three simple quatrains with alternate lines rhyming. Deceptively light in form and throw-away in tone (despite the initial shock of the opening line), it utters a fundamental truth about hereditary influence. Quite simply, the theme is that the 'faults' – he means hereditary traits – are passed on by parents to children unwittingly, and that this is extended, by their own behaviour, to create additional ones. The second verse looks back beyond to the influence of the parents' parents ('fools in old-style hats and coats') whose inconsistency made for suffering in their children. The third verse is the ultimate in cynicism, with the simile in its second line using a natural phenomenon as an illustration of human nature. The final line, climatic to the poem, contains the simple advice or injunction not to get involved in having children yourself. It is a wry, dry, laconic pronouncement, but the cynicism is inlaid with humour. The title of the poem is ironic too I feel – perhaps a kind of 'The reading for today ...' It is from R. L. Stevenson's 'Requiem' – 'This be the verse you grave for me.'

## Vers de Société

First of all, note the regular verse form; each has six lines, with the rhymes varied according to the ease, freedom and fluency required. Verse one has three rhyming couplets, with three lines end-stopped for emphasis, definite statement. In the second verse the couplets are enclosed by the first and sixth lines, which rhyme, and thereafter there are variants in each of the verses. In the last verse the poet returns to the form of the first, a subtle way of showing that he is returning to the problem – of whether to accept the invitation or not. The running-on of each verse into the next conveys the anxious circling thoughts in the thinker's own mind. The tone is colloquial, relaxed, ironic; the title itself is ironic too, as we see from Margaret Drabble's definition of the genre: 'a form of light verse dealing with events in polite society, usually in a satiric or playful tone, sometimes conversational, sometimes employing intricate forms.' Larkin uses quite an intricate form, but is often impolite. The theme is not light but serious and, in a way, typical of Larkin.

The direct response at the beginning (and the satire of the invitation itself) speaks the truth instead of purveying the customary hypocritical politeness. The second half of the third line is coarse and unequivocal, perhaps politely translated as 'I would enjoy coming to your party about as much as I would like being stuck up a pig's anus'. The next two lines show the writer alone, while the last (of the first verse) has him mentally beginning a rejection. The second verse underlines time which is wasted, for him, on social occasions, and the colloquialisms are strengthened by the unusual use of 'canted', the irony of 'washing sherry' and of consumer concern, seen in the reference to the magazine *Which*. The third verse has the fine alliterative linking of 'forks and faces', as if they represent for the poet the undesirable form of socializing; being alone on the other hand can mean reading, studying, observing, which constitute *real* living (as far as he is concerned). Here 'air-sharpened' is an unusual, suggestive coinage which evokes freedom. The light verse now assumes a moral tone; it is supposedly selfish to be solitary, virtuous to be sociable. There is an ironic implication that religion has decayed too. Moreover, socializing puts you on a treadmill of having to keep it up, of repaying being entertained in the same way. The fifth verse explores the motives of this, of our being made to feel obliged to play at the ritual of social observance and to be seen doing it. In the sixth verse there is a note of pathos. When you are young you 'can be alone freely', for at that time you have not acquired social obligations (and studying is required of you). As you get older, loneliness brings 'other things', for example the unvoiced fear (of death we feel) and self-contemplation of our errors. In the end, as here, we conform – accept the invitations. We are caught in the trap of social activity, hence the title of the poem. Note the subtle use of the word 'Warlock' in the name – for the poet, socializing is a witch's ritual – but note too that the fear so often present in Larkin emerges in the last verse. Despite the light-verse tone there is some serious contemplation in the poem. In the end is the beginning, cunningly reversed. In the end we conform, doing what we are expected to do. It is an escape from the apprehensions we feel within us.

*craps* Worthless people, a waste of time.
*Warlock* Male witch (but Larkin is perhaps also despising the double-barrelled name here).
*canted* Leaning, but punning on hypocritical and trite conversation.
*Which* The magazine of the Consumers' Association.

## Cut Grass

A beautiful, lyrical, moving and sad poem. The short lines with alternate ones rhyming show the quality of the poet's control, and throughout there is a fine, sure, running alliteration. The focus gives the reader the sense of physical wounding, as well as the wounding of the senses which one gets from the word-pictures. The flow of the first verse into the second seems an indication of the time it takes the grass to die. The double-barrelled 'young-leafed' provides effective contrast to the death. Sound and light cohere to make beautiful rhythmic pictures. The sights are blended, and the cloud here does not carry an ominous suggestion, despite the earlier death-images of the poem.

*Cut Grass* The title is taken from the passage in the Prayer Book of 1662: '. . . the grass. In the morning it is green and groweth up, but in the evening it is cut down and withered'.
*white . . .* Note the repetition of this adjective, white for youth, innocence and also for what is insubstantial.
*Queen Anne's lace* Wild flower of the carrot family, it has large lacy flowers.

## Forget What Did

Six three-line verses, with some half-rhymes and consonance. The title indicates the determination to put out of one's mind what happened in life. The abbreviated phrase, which eliminates the word 'happen', shows that the practice has already started. The sound of the words in the first verse reflects the strength and effect of this decision ('Stopping', 'stun', 'starting'), and 'blank' anticipates the pages which will never be filled in. The suggestion is that you injure yourself by recording in words a day from waking onwards, and here 'cicatrized' is a vivid and unusual usage. The third and fourth verses concentrate on looking back, with the period of youth here coinciding with that of wars. 'Opaque' suggests blinkered (remember Larkin's own short-sightedness). He then queries what will happen to the unfilled pages, and suggests that nothing personal should be entered. The 'celestial recurrences' (sunset, phases of the moon) could be recorded, but the last two lines of the poem contain a superb duality. On one level they mean the period of spring (flowers) and of autumn ('when the birds go'), but they also suggest, I believe, death, funeral, end of natural life. Larkin often injects a personal poignancy at the end of a poem.

**cicatrized** Scarred.
**Celestial recurrences** See the comment above, but also note that the reference may be to spiritual rather than material things.

## Livings

I
This has obvious points of connection with 'Friday Night in the Royal Station Hotel'. The form is a relaxed *ottava rima*, each of the verses ending in a rhyming couplet. The tone is first-person conversational, the man concerned being a salesman who sells 'things like dip and feed'. Again the theme is loneliness, the deadly monotony of his life being described, much of it in the flat statements which echo his existence. Again the broken lines so often employed by Larkin convey the small, habitual details which constitute these ritual trips to the hotel. In the third verse there is the wonderful poetic lift of the sky seeming 'like the bed/Of a gold river', and the accompanying uplifting realization that, for a moment, the salesman himself sees something beyond

his own limited horizons. The contemplative last few lines place the poem in time, but underline how reluctant we are to change from one routine to another, even if that first routine is a form of stagnation.

## II

Six verses of five lines each, again blank verse lines, brief, pungent, evocative. The blunt, freer form of II conveys, perhaps, the greater freedom and naturalness of the lighthouse-keeper's way of life, in contrast to the other two 'livings'. In verse one the lighthouse-keeper looks down from his high vantage point. Verse two maintains the perspective, with a fine line ('Husband their tenacity') and the moving acknowledgement (not unlike the Ancient Mariner's) of love for the 'Creatures', the only living (echo of the title) things near him. Verse three is superbly compact, with the sea compared to fields and the personified contact of the radio, again moving because of the keeper's isolation. What the radio says, wonderful in its range, is reported in verse four, while verse five returns to what he is surrounded by at night. The inside-outside contrast vivifies the final verse, with the loneliness of eating by himself (though 'Guarded by brilliance' – the light) and selecting cards foretelling the future offset by the imaginative description of the liners and their movement from his perspective. Larkin has many outsider/loner poems of mood; this one is a 'living' fact.

## III

This 'living', set back into the eighteenth century in a college (Oxford or Cambridge), is written in three eight-line verses which have alternate lines rhyming. The tone is first-person narrative (as are the other two in the sequence) and despite the culture-gap we are reminded of 'The Card-Players' through the vivid picturing of this leisured, cultured – and crude – company. The conversation, with its dated references, helps to fix the period. Drinking, pissing, argument after heavy eating and discussion, these are the mainsprings of verse two. Verse three ranges over the perspective outside the room, just as the previous two poems did. As one might expect, because of its location this poem has learned and cultivated associations.

**the boots** The member of staff at a hotel who cleans the boots and shoes.

**single** Single bedroom.

**taking the knock** Suffering financially.

**Husband their tenacity** Conserve their ability to cling to the rocks.

**Radio rubs its legs** The crackling of the radio reminds the narrator of crickets or grasshoppers rubbing their legs together to communicate.

**Fires in humped inns . . .** 'humped'. to protect themselves from cold and wind. The smoke from their fires gives a thin film over the sea pictures, making them like kippers which are hung over a fire to be smoked.

**(O loose moth world)** A deliberate echo of 'O brave new world' (*The Tempest*). The contrast here is effective because there is no 'beauteous mankind' but formless snow, floating (like moths), ethereal until the hard, biting presence of the last two lines.

**Nocturnal vapours** i.e. night breezes (from which he might take a chill) or, more likely, evening drinking which would upset his health.

**advowson** The right of presentation, the gift of a vacant benefice or living to the most suitable person.

**Snape** Small town inland from Aldeburgh in Suffolk.

*pudendum mulieris* The female genitalia (Latin).

**Judas** Judas Iscariot, the disciple who betrayed Christ.

**Jack Ketch** A celebrated hangman, the public executioner who died in 1686.

**Starveling** The tailor in Shakespeare's *A Midsummer Night's Dream* (Archaic meaning is 'someone ill-fed'.)

**jordan** Chamber-pot.

**bogs** Lavatories.

**rheumy fevers** Rheumatism, rheumatic fevers.

**Regicide** The killing of a king, or the person who does the killing.

**sizar** At Peterhouse, Cambridge and Trinity College, Dublin – a student who is maintained by his college.

**Chaldean constellations** The Chaldeans were a race who ruled Babylon, noted for their wise men, astrologers, magicians. This term therefore embraces the wisdom and knowledge of the heavens, perhaps an ironic contrast with that within the University.


## Going, Going

Nine verses of six lines each, conversational and colloquial and confiding the poet's worries about the taking over of the England he has known by increasing consumerism and urbaniz-ation, with the consequent loss of the countryside and culture. The first verse (regular rhyme scheme throughout) describes the poet's feeling that there would never be real change, that at least in his lifetime things would remain as they were. The second verse records some urban encroachments ('bleak high-risers') but the countryside was still within reach. Verse three begins with the idea of nature surviving anything, but at the end doubt nags at him as he sees all the evidence of the consumer society around him. This spans simple greed and sophisticated takeover and expansion into the hitherto protected rural areas. We now see clearly the suggestion inherent in the title – England is under the auctioneer's hammer and will soon be sold (gone) to the highest bidders. In the sixth verse the real fear of the speed at which this is all happening is emphasized by the break in line two. The language in the seventh verse is unequivocally outspoken: England will become 'First slum of Europe'. For the poet this urbanization consists of buildings and cars (verse eight) while the pessimistic finality of verse nine traces the decline as inevitable. The language is low-key, often clichéd, its monotony, and the monotony of the verses, reflecting the terrible monotony of life to come.

**bleak high-risers** Blocks of flats, perhaps up to twenty storeys high.
**snuff it** Slang for 'die'.
**the whole Boiling** Everything, the lot (from sweet-making, where all ingredients are put in to boil together).
**a role . . .** Dramatic metaphor indicating that the country is seeking the limelight of disgrace.
**tarts** Loose women, prostitutes.
**guildhalls** Meeting places for members of guilds or trades.
**carved choirs** Wooden pews in a church set aside for choirs.

## The Building

There are nine seven-line verses with a pattern of rhyme, half-rhyme and consonance; the title is a euphemism for 'hospital'. The tone is a little more elevated than usual, perhaps because of the nature of the subject. The surround is factually drawn (rather like the scenes of 'The Whitsun Weddings') and again there is poetic elevation, as, for instance, in 'Like a great sigh out of the last century'. The use of the negative, as so often in Larkin, tells us so much, like 'not taxis'. The 'frightening smell' which is characteristic of hospitals suggests disinfectant and the indefinable smell of death. Verse two is factual, though the 'airport lounge' image is ominous with innuendo, since some will soon be taking off for death. The description of faces traces the spectrum from acceptance to apprehension which is revealed in people who attend a hospital. The mechanical actions of those waiting are recaptured in verse three. The stress on 'The end of choice' is an idea shared with 'The Old Fools', since illness takes freedom away from us. The idea of 'confess' (present in 'Ambulances') is also taken up. The fact 'that something has gone wrong' with the body which has to be 'confessed' to the doctor provides a kind of physical/spiritual link. That illness happens at any time is also stressed. The journey upwards marks the space, but each room is a space in which to die. In verse six there is another look outside (a reminder again of the technique in 'The Whitsun Weddings') which is almost a restoring of perspective. These outside descriptions employ dated slang ('hairdos'). The divisions between dream outside and reality inside are stressed in verse seven, while the eighth stays firmly inside, the patients seen ironically as 'congregations' (worshipping what?). The end of the verse sees them all as 'coin' – human currency which gains you admission to the hospital. The payment is for death, whether now or later. The hospital is a 'clean-sliced cliff' (you might compare this with the 'alp' of 'The Old Fools'). There is no answer to death, nothing to stop it. The visitors to the sick and dying are seen as pathetically offering flowers, 'propitiatory' in the hope of a response, or of saving. Note the finality of the final single, separated line, symbolizing the cut-off state of the patients. It is a moving poem, encapsulating the Larkin obsession with death.

**lucent comb** i.e. brightly lit, with several layers (or teeth).
**those who tamely sit ... haven't come far** Ironic, since in many cases they haven't far to go.
**ripped mags** Torn magazines.
**separates** Outfits made up of separate parts, e.g. blouses and skirts or tops and trousers, designed to be worn separately or together.

## The Old Fools

The poem has a fine rhetorical flourish about it. There are eleven and a half lines to each verse, with a regular rhyme scheme throughout the four verses. The long verses and lines make for a conversational tone. Questions which are unanswerable are asked. The obsession is with the onset of old age and its effects. Examples are loss of memory and incontinence. Again

Larkin here adapts a proverbial phrase – 'There's no fool like an old fool' – for this dotage is really the second childhood of senility. The tone, though critical and laced with a kind of bitterness, continues to ask the unanswerable – do the old really believe they could become what they once were? Their youth is pathetically invoked, but remember that the poet is outside *their* experience and is angry at their state – and fears that he will one day be the same. The first verse covers past experiences, while 'Watching light move' is expressive of their present vacancy. The second verse is a direct factual account of what happens at death; it then moves on to suggest at one and the same time the miracle of creation and the blowing up of everything. There is the idea, I feel, of the complexity of the human body and the mind, the making of the atom bomb. We shall end up in 'oblivion' anyway. Notice the effect of the negatives towards the end of this verse – the loss of choice for example – and the repugnant physical effects of the last line which suggest the decay of the body. The third verse shows the poet's imagination at work on the idea of life going on in the mind but lacking outside communication. The poem is informed with the fear which is made explicit at the very end. In this third verse, though, sights, habits and memories recur in a dislocated way, conveyed by the punctuation which gives a stuttery effect. The implication is that the old are perhaps 'living' in a past which cannot be integrated into the present, and this accounts for the vacancy. All this is surmise, and this inwardness must degenerate too as they get nearer death. To the poet the fact that they don't appear to register a reaction to death is cause for further anger and exclamation, and he ranges over the idea that they must surely recognize it – in lonely wakings, for instance. The 'hideous inverted childhood' is a bitter definition of their state. The last line, typically and laconically Larkin, is heavily ironic. 'We shall find out' is effective because it means both that it will happen to us and we won't have the sense left to understand it anyway. The long flowing lines of the poem are another successful blending of form and content being brought appropriately together: the length reflects the length of life and, for some, the long period of senility before death. Anger, bitterness, frustration, the sense of an inevitability which cannot be fought, all these characterize this poem.

**pissing**  Urinating (through incontinence).
**sloped arms**  Part of Army rifle drill.
**Ash hair**  Thin and grey like the trunk of the ash-tree (and looking
  forward punningly to the 'ashes' after cremation).

## Money

A poem of four quatrains, each having two rhyming couplets.
The first verse covers the money used to pay quarterly bills,
suggesting that it could have been – and still could be – used for
material goods and sex. The theme here is that we ought to
make use of what we have never fully made use of. The second
verse shows the writer in self-deprecating mood. In easy colloquial phrases he spells out the rewards to be gained from money
in the consumer society, the equation of material goods with
marriage being part of the humorous comment. The third verse
takes up the previous verse's third line, with the idea that money
and life go together; you should live (and therefore spend) while
you can, since saving ultimately achieves nothing. The last verse
has what Larkin's poetry so often has, a poignancy of tone and
contemplation. The comparison with the town, the contemplation of the mixture in life, is complemented by the inherent
sadness and recognition that money and life do go together in
the terrible sense that either you have it or you don't have it. The
statement 'intensely sad' conveys the strength of feeling; the
irony embraces the extremes, the poverty of the slums, the
wealth of the church. There is a fine imaginative usage – the
idea of money 'singing', the use of the word 'mad' (note carefully
what it means), and the throwaway colloquial 'screw'.

**screw**  Slang term for wages, salary.

## Show Saturday

This is a long poem by Larkin standards, and it has distinctively
long lines, rhythmically controlled, with something of the
flavour of a poet Larkin greatly admired, John Betjeman. The
verses are of eight lines each with alternate lines rhyming. The
first verse describes the scene at the beginning of the show, the
observation finely selective in a series of word-pictures. The lines
here and in verse two are broken to give the maximum effect to
the statements, the poet's overview being something like the

sweep of a camera. Incidents, like the wrestling, are vividly described in the third verse, while the vegetables and food on display occupy verse four. Verse five continues inside then moves outside, impressions being recorded surely as the poet registers them. The verses unwind just as the Saturday of the show unwinds. By the end of the sixth verse the show is at an end, and the last two verses describe the return of those attending to their various homes. Their lives, occupations are recorded, but the tone of the final verse, which follows the semi-humorous survey of the show and its effects, contains a plea for the annual regeneration of this ritual. It will surface every year, and people will hardly notice the onset of changes in themselves and others; this last emphasis shows the customary Larkin awareness of death. The poem alternates between relatively factual description, vivid images and ironic contemplation of what has happened. The variants in the rhyme scheme make for flexibility.

**Cheviot and Blackface** Hill breeds of sheep.
**a man with pound notes ... a lit-up board** One of the many who appear at shows and run games of chance, gamblers.
**Like great straw dice** Note the effectiveness of the simile which emphasizes that for many it is a gambling day.
**pure excellences ...** This seems to mean that the skills involved in growing and cooking are on the decrease and will not be passed on.
**sports finals** The editions of sports papers giving the final results.
**saddle-swank** i.e. showing off their riding skills.

## Revision questions on *High Windows*

1 Write an appreciation of the title poem in this sequence.

2 By reference to any two poems, show how Larkin considers himself to be an outsider.

3 By reference to any two poems, show that Larkin is a good descriptive poet.

4 Show how Larkin employs a conversational tone in any of these poems.

5 Which poem in this sequence do you consider to be typical of Larkin and why?

**6** Bring out the humour or the cynicism in any three or four poems.

**7** How important is a sense of place in Larkin's poetry? Refer to any two or three poems in your answer.

**8** Write a detailed appreciation of either 'The Card-Players' or two sections from 'Livings'.

**9** Which poem in this sequence do you consider to be the most unusual and why?

**10** Write an appreciation of the poem you have enjoyed most in this group.

# General questions

1 **Write an appreciation of any Larkin poem which you consider brings out the main qualities of his verse.**

*Suggested notes for essay answer* (It is obviously a free choice, but here is a possible approach to 'The Whitsun Weddings'.)
(a) Introduction: the form of the poem – Larkin's sensitivity to form (quote other poems) – what form does here. (b) Bring out tone of poem: conversational – description – word-pictures – journey – contemporary life (refer to another poem on contemporary life) (c) Atmosphere: inside outside – economy – urban-country associations; *then* observation of weddings – detail – ironic humour – factual reportage – description *then* (d) Contemplation: end of journey beginning of another journey – coincidence – symbolism at the conclusion of the poem. (e) Summarize main Larkin techniques/attitudes in conclusion – stress language, description, irony, close observation, tone, symbolism.

2 Compare and contrast two poems written at different stages in Larkin's life and say what you have most enjoyed about them.

3 Write an appreciation of three short Larkin poems where he employs colloquial language and cliché.

4 Write an essay on Larkin's use of symbolism in his verse.

5 Is Larkin merely a cynical, depressing poet? Write an essay for or against this view, referring to at least four poems in your answer.

6 Which of Larkin's poems seem to you lyrical and why?

7 What do you learn of Larkin's attitudes to life from his poetry? Refer to four or five poems in your answer.

8 'He is obsessed by the thought of death.' How far would you agree or disagree with this statement?

9 Discuss Larkin's attitudes towards either (a) being sociable or (b) personal relationships in any selection of his poems.

10 In which of his poems do you think Larkin uses satire most successfully?

**11** Larkin believed that poetry should be readily understood. Do you feel that you understand his poems? Give reasons for your answer.

**12** Discuss Larkin's use of monologue or dialogue or both in selected poems.

**13** In what ways is Larkin a descriptive poet? Refer to two or three poems in your answer.

**14** 'Often, he just sets out to shock.' How far would you agree with this assessment of Larkin's verse?

**15** It has been said that in his best poems he tells a story. Write an appreciation of any two or three of Larkin's story-poems.

**16** What do you think Larkin enjoyed most in life? Refer to two or three poems in support of your views.

# Further reading

At the time of writing, there are a few studies of Larkin's poetry which would be of direct help:

*Larkin* by Roger Day (Open Guides to Literature, Open University Press, 1987). An excellent study, with close examination of particular poems and student participation and involvement at every stage.

*Philip Larkin* by Andrew Motion (Routledge, 1982). An excellent all-round introduction to the complete works. Motion is writing Larkin's biography.

*Philip Larkin (1922–1985) A Tribute*, edited by George Hartley (The Marvell Press, 1988). A number of poems and some useful essays on aspects of Larkin's art. No index, and the comments on individual poems vary greatly from the esoteric and academic to the trivial and self-conscious. But worth a close look.

*An Enormous Yes: in memoriam Philip Larkin*, edited by Harry Chambers (Peterloo Poets, 1986). As above, and including some Larkin poems and statements.

*The Whitsun Weddings and The Less Deceived* by Andrew Swarbrick (Macmillan Master Guides, 1986). Intelligent, sensitive examination of individual poems and a good introduction to Larkin's art.

Students may be interested to read other works by Larkin, such as:
*Jill* and *A Girl in Winter*, both novels.

*All What Jazz: A record Diary*, 1961–71.
*Required Writing: Miscellaneous Pieces* 1955–82 (All Faber and Faber).

Individual collections are published by Faber and Faber and *The Less Deceived* by The Marvell Press.

*Philip Larkin: Collected Poems*, edited with an introduction by Anthony Thwaite (The Marvell Press and Faber and Faber, 1988), is essential reading.

# Index of titles

# Brodie's Notes

TITLES IN THE SERIES

| | |
|---|---|
| D. H. Lawrence | **The Rainbow** |
| D. H. Lawrence | **Sons and Lovers** |
| D. H. Lawrence | **Women in Love** |
| Harper Lee | **To Kill a Mockingbird** |
| Laurie Lee | **Cider with Rosie** |
| Christopher Marlowe | **Dr Faustus** |
| Arthur Miller | **The Crucible** |
| Arthur Miller | **Death of a Salesman** |
| John Milton | **Paradise Lost, Books I and II** |
| Robert C. O'Brien | **Z for Zachariah** |
| Sean O'Casey | **Juno and the Paycock** |
| George Orwell | **Animal Farm** |
| George Orwell | **1984** |
| J. B. Priestley | **An Inspector Calls** |
| J. D. Salinger | **The Catcher in the Rye** |
| William Shakespeare | **Antony and Cleopatra** |
| William Shakespeare | **As You Like It** |
| William Shakespeare | **Hamlet** |
| William Shakespeare | **Henry IV Part I** |
| William Shakespeare | **Henry IV Part II** |
| William Shakespeare | **Julius Caesar** |
| William Shakespeare | **King Lear** |
| William Shakespeare | **Macbeth** |
| William Shakespeare | **Measure for Measure** |
| William Shakespeare | **The Merchant of Venice** |
| William Shakespeare | **A Midsummer Night's Dream** |
| William Shakespeare | **Much Ado about Nothing** |
| William Shakespeare | **Othello** |
| William Shakespeare | **Richard II** |
| William Shakespeare | **Richard III** |
| William Shakespeare | **Romeo and Juliet** |
| William Shakespeare | **The Tempest** |
| William Shakespeare | **Twelfth Night** |
| George Bernard Shaw | **Pygmalion** |
| Alan Sillitoe | **Selected Fiction** |
| John Steinbeck | **Of Mice and Men** and **The Pearl** |
| Jonathan Swift | **Gulliver's Travels** |
| Dylan Thomas | **Under Milk Wood** |
| Alice Walker | **The Color Purple** |
| W. B. Yeats | **Selected Poetry** |

## ENGLISH COURSEWORK BOOKS

| | |
|---|---|
| Terri Apter | **Women and Society** |
| Kevin Dowling | **Drama and Poetry** |
| Philip Gooden | **Conflict** |
| Philip Gooden | **Science Fiction** |
| Margaret K. Gray | **Modern Drama** |
| Graham Handley | **Modern Poetry** |
| Graham Handley | **Prose** |
| Graham Handley | **Childhood and Adolescence** |
| R. J. Sims | **The Short Story** |